THE DO-IT-YOURSELF LOBOTOMY

Adweek Books is designed to present interesting, insightful books for the general business reader and for professionals in the worlds of media, marketing, and advertising.

These are innovative, creative books that address the challenges and opportunities of these industries, written by leaders in the business. Some of our writers head their own companies, others have worked their way up to the top of their field in large multinationals. But they share a knowledge of their craft and a desire to enlighten others.

We hope readers will find these books as helpful and inspiring as *Adweek, Brandweek,* and *Mediaweek* magazines.

Published

Disruption: Overturning Conventions and Shaking Up the Marketplace, Jean-Marie Dru

Under the Radar: Talking to Today's Cynical Consumer, Jonathan Bond and Richard Kirshenbaum

Truth, Lies and Advertising: The Art of Account Planning, Jon Steel

Hey, Whipple, Squeeze This: A Guide to Creating Great Ads, Luke Sullivan

Eating the Big Fish: How Challenger Brands Can Compete Against Brand Leaders, Adam Morgan

Warp-Speed Branding: The Impact of Technology on Marketing, Agnieszka Winkler

Creative Company: How St. Luke's Became "the Ad Agency to End All Ad Agencies," Andy Law

Another One Bites the Grass: Making Sense of International Advertising, Simon Anholt

Attention! How to Interrupt, Yell, Whisper and Touch Consumers, Ken Sacharin

The Peaceable Kingdom: Building a Company without Factionalism, Fiefdoms, Fear, and Other Staples of Modern Business, Stan Richards with David Culp

Getting the Bugs Out: The Rise, Fall, and Comeback of Volkswagen in America, by David Kiley

Forthcoming

Beyond Disruption: Changing the Rules in the Marketplace by Jean-Marie Dru

And Now a Few Laughs From Our Sponsor by Larry Oakner

THE
DO-IT-YOURSELF
LOBOTOMY

Open Your Mind to Greater
Creative Thinking

Tom Monahan

John Wiley & Sons, Inc.

This book is dedicated to
the five most important people in my life: my wife,
my best friend, my honey, my partner, and my soul mate.

Of course, that would be Audrey.

Contents

PART I

What Do Great Ideas Do?

Introduction

Ideas First!

One thing is certain:

> *To survive, to thrive in business in the twenty-first century you need to be a potent idea generator.*

Whether you're in advertising, high finance, technology, funeral management, or any other field, every big idea that has ever helped your industry was the result of creative thinking. Every solution to every real problem has come from a new idea. Every triumph over every challenge and every gain from every opportunity has been the result of an individual stretching her or his gray matter to a new and valuable place.

Great ideas are the root of just about everything new. Every new product, service improvement, cost savings, and efficiency idea has come from human creativeness. Every market-conquering, competition-smashing concept behind every advancement is the result of someone thinking of something that has not been thought of before.

The vital, urgent need for constant creative thinking is as pervasive in industry today as computer terminals and interminable meetings.

Creative thinking is no longer the domain of a chosen few or something companies do only at their annual planning meetings or in brainstorming sessions. Creative thinking is something that high-functioning people at leading companies do constantly, because there is always an opportunity for improvement. Today, with the pace of change constantly increasing in business, there is always a need to maintain a competitive advantage. Companies and individuals both need to stay on top of their game.

So where do creative ideas come from? Well . . . people. The freshest, biggest ideas come from leaders in your own industry and other industries. Ideas also come from the customers and users of your goods or services. And if your company is a player to any degree and you're doing your job, creative ideas come from *you*. (If you're a manager doing your job, they also come from your people.)

Now is the time to ask yourself, "What am I doing to enable myself and/or my people to generate the vital business-building ideas that fuel my company's, my clients', and our customers' success?"

Take a second to let that question sink in.

Now answer honestly, "What are you doing, now, to become a better idea generator?"

> *If you're not making a concerted effort to value, master, and inspire creative thinking and improve your skill set in this area, you may find yourself losing out to the competition.*

If you don't actively grease the skids of innovation and better handle the rapidity and magnitude of change today, you could be cheating yourself and your employer out of an incredible resource. You could be holding back your company and your career.

Fresh ideas are the lubrication for growth and success in business. Whether it's creative marketing ideas, breakthrough advertising ideas, customer service ideas, or fresh thinking in a thousand other areas, the most successful people in business are making themselves active players in this high-stakes, high-value game.

You're reading this book because you want to improve yourself in this area. I can help you. As a professional creative thinking coach I work with thousands of people in dozens of industry segments annually to help them improve their understanding and skills in this critical area. My experience tells me that it's helpful early on in this self-development process to take a quick personal inventory of your current state of creativeness.

SELF-ASSESSMENT FOR SELF-IMPROVEMENT

How potent is your idea power? Are you and/or your people able to come up with an abundance of tremendously creative ideas when you need them with little effort or pain? Dozens of ideas? Hundreds of ideas? Thousands of ideas? Well, there's a lot more method to this madness than most people realize (or perhaps, madness to the method). And it's surprisingly easy to accomplish.

To help make this learning process more meaningful and therefore more effective for you individually, here are some self-diagnostic tools.

> *The 2-minute Creative IQ Test*, page 238. (Or for a more interactive version go to www.Do-It-YourselfLobotomy.com/book.) By "Creative IQ" I mean your *imagination quotient*. I have developed this assessment tool to help people determine the areas in which they are already strong creatively and those that need improvement—and how much. This quick little test, taken by thousands of people, has been developed and refined based on a great deal of feedback. It's the most popular page at my web site. I have gotten hundreds of comments from people telling me how they have used this little tool to better understand their creative strengths and weaknesses so they can take charge of their self-improvement in this area. I suggest you take this short test before you get too far along in the book. The assessment will help you focus on the chapters that will benefit you most.
>
> *The 2-minute Organizational Creative IQ Test*, page 246. (Or go to www.Do-It-YourselfLobotomy.com/book.) This quick diagnostic tool is for assessing the creative health of the people in your organization as a group. If you're a manager reading this book as much to help you bring out creativity in the people you supervise as for your own professional and personal development, this little test is well worth a look. It will help you better understand areas that need to be worked on at an organizational level, whether they be team, department, division, or company.

Creative ForceField Analysis, page 251. (Or for a more interactive version go to www.Do-It-YourselfLobotomy.com/book.) This self-diagnostic tool will help you identify factors that encourage creativeness in your life on the positive side of your "Creative ForceField" and those that prevent or limit creativity on the negative side. In my years as a consultant, I have used this tool often to assess individuals and organizations. We almost always use it as a road map to help us identify the stuck places before doing our work together. We sometimes use the exact same tool after the professional development work to identify the positive shifts that were made. Again, I suggest you use this tool to create a benchmark of sorts before you get too far along in the book. I suggest you do it again, or just edit your original version, after you've read the book. You'll be amazed at how much awareness alone can help increase your creative forcefield. You can do it as an individual or to assess your organization's Creative ForceField.

KNOWLEDGE ⓘⓈ POWER

This book is about empowerment. But not in the touchy-feely 1980s sense of giving yourself permission to be your best self, although you certainly had better be doing that. True empowerment means giving yourself the understanding and resources to make major contributions to your industry, your company, and your self-worth.

> *The great irony of the information age is that knowledge is not as powerful as it used to be.*

There was a time on this planet when only a few people had knowledge, and they held the power. The monarchy, the church, the aristocracy—those few who had the knowledge and education had the power. Today we are a more educated society. And what we don't know we can often find out with the click of a mouse. Just a few short years ago in the halls of business we often heard the term *proprietary information.* What's proprietary today? And for how long? All companies have access to the same information.

WHAT KIND OF THINKER
DO YOU WANT TO BE?

Do you want to be the kind of thinker who comes up with the idea of a personal computer with a larger hard drive and faster processor just like everyone else was doing in the late 1990s? Or do you want to be the kind of thinker who comes up with the idea that made iMac the top selling personal computer for two years running? It wasn't faster. It wasn't bigger. It was blue. Excuse me, blueberry.

Do you want to be a thinker who develops one more in a long line of shampoos that gives your hair "longer-lasting body?" Or do you want to be the thinker who understands that people standing in a shower wait impatiently for the gooey shampoo to come out of a bottle and decides to put the cap on the *bottom* of the bottle, like Pantene?

Do you want to be the thinker who comes up with one more commercial for a high-technology company that talks about "integrating your IT services"? Or do you want to be the thinker who decides to show nuns speaking French on American TV, discussing their processor speed and hard drive size and making one of the largest, monolithic companies in the world, IBM, seem down-to-earth by offering "solutions for a small planet"?

Do you want to be the thinker who comes up with one more variety of packaged guacamole, loaded with artery-clogging fat like all the

An easy-to-recognize example of 180° Thinking (see page 99).

other avocado-based guacamole? Or do you want to be a thinker who asks, "Does guacamole have to be made from avocado?" then goes on to use asparagus as the main ingredient to invent a great-tasting no-fat guacamole like Espárrago zesty asparagus guacamole?

Do you want to be one more in a long line of aerospace engineers who thinks of a way to make jets faster? Or do you want to be the thinker whose huge idea finally made the Stealth bomber virtually invisible to radar? An idea that wasn't about technology. An idea that wasn't about aerodynamics. An idea that was about slowing down the speed of the craft so that the heat output would be diminished to an acceptable non-radar-reflective point.

These are all examples of people who did not go with the flow of conventional thinking. Some who even defied the status quo. A computer that is not faster! Guacamole that doesn't contain any avocado! An advanced jet that functions best going slower!

Ideas like these and just about every other fresh concept that contributes to progress in every field of endeavor happen when people let go of what they "know," when they "lobotomize" the part of their brain that already has the "right" answer and come up with a better idea.

Are you ready to perform a Do-It-Yourself Lobotomy™?

❖

The power today goes to those who can act quickly on the knowledge by using new ideas to gain an edge—an edge that lets you lean back and enjoy its fruits for a very short time, as your competitors brainstorm to gain *their* edge.

That is the aim of this book. To truly empower your creative resourcefulness. To give you the ability to come up with as many big, fresh ideas as you wish, when you wish, with little effort or pain. To be able to think like the biggest thinkers in your field. To actually be a leader in your field.

Follow the advice, the lessons, and the methodologies in this book and you'll be better equipped than your competitors to deal with the challenges and convert the opportunities that face you every day. Because in business today, creativity is not a luxury—it is absolutely essential to success.

Knowledge versus New Ideas

You go to school, you gain knowledge. You join the workforce, you learn more. As you claw your way up the corporate ladder, you keep filling your mind with information—facts, data, understanding.

"Knowledge is power," you're told. Daily you strive to know as much about your field as possible to be competitive, to have an edge, to gain success.

But who gains the greatest success in business? Those who cram existing knowledge into their brains? Or those who generate the new ideas, the fresh thinking, the creative sparks that ignite new areas of business growth?

At a point in most every high-achieving professional's career he or she makes a profound discovery. The greatest success comes not from memorizing and processing other people's ideas, but in conceiving, giving birth to, and bringing to maturity their own ideas.

> A great many people think they are thinking when they are merely rearranging prejudices.
>
> William James

For many people, finding truly new ideas is not nearly as easy as it seems. Most people in business, while seeing the value of original thinking, find it extremely difficult to achieve. As a professional creative thinking coach, I understand this problem better than most people in business. I work with thousands of businesspeople annually: professionals in all corners of the corporate world and beyond, in Fortune 500 companies, in ad agencies of all sizes, in small firms, in professional organizations, one-on-one, and everywhere in between. I see that, in spite of their sincere intentions, most people are prisoners of what they know and are virtually helpless when it comes to generating new ideas. Their minds have become enslaved by traditional thinking: "the way it's done," "the tried and true," "the known." Their grooves of thought lead them to the same place time and again. The world around them is changing at breakneck speed, but they are stuck in the traps of old thinking patterns, being run over by those few players who are unattached to the old and are creating the new.

⋘✦⋙

HOW THE DO-IT-YOURSELF LOBOTOMY WILL HELP YOU

The Do-It-Yourself Lobotomy will help you let go of your preconceptions, enabling you to have fresh ideas whenever you need or want them.

- First we help you better *understand creativity*, because you can't master something you don't truly understand. We cover some of the fundamental concepts about creativeness that are sorely misunderstood:

Creativity = problem solving. We can either let problems be barriers or use them as springboards to be at our creative best when solving problems (see page 49).

Change. At best, most people go with the flow of change; at worst, they resist it. The high achievers *effect* change. You certainly can't avoid change, at least on this planet, today or ever (see page 57).

Creativity versus talent. These are very different notions. Not everyone is talented artistically. But everyone has the ability to have new ideas (see pag 62).

- Next we help you isolate the basic *creative thinking tools*, the methods and techniques used by the greatest thinkers since the beginning of time.

  Ask a Better Question™ (see page 75)

  100 MPH Thinking™ (see page 90)

  180° Thinking™ (see page 99)

  Intergalactic Thinking™ (see page 107)

- Finally, we help you gain deeper perspectives on *other aspects of creativity* to help you apply your new lessons to your job and life, to help you produce big ideas to fuel your success and that of your company.

❖

THE CREATIVE EDGE (DOUBLE-EDGE, THAT IS)

I've helped over 100,000 people in business to "grease their minds," in the words of one of my clients. In my corporate work, in both training and the applied-creativity world of brainstorm facilitation, I have worked with professionals in hundreds of companies, including Virgin Atlantic Airways, Hasbro, Frito-Lay, Texas Instruments, Benjamin Moore, and Capital One, as well as a large percentage of the top advertising agencies in the world. Through this work I have developed and refined ways to enable people to let go of what they know and to free their minds to discover new and better ways of doing their jobs, fueling their companies, and boosting their careers.

At the core of all of the work I do is a fun, fast-paced, precept-shattering workshop that I call "The Do-It-Yourself Lobotomy." That

How the Do-It-Yourself Lobotomy Works

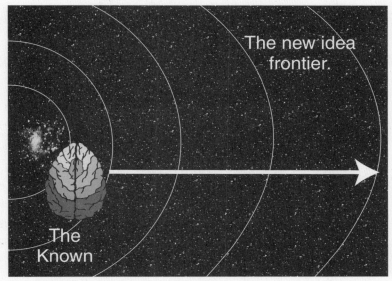

Conventional thinking and problem solving is like white light. By the very nature of logical, linear thinking, you illuminate only what you aim at.

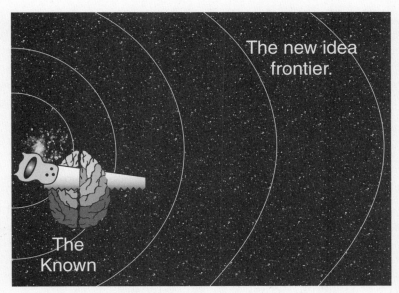

The Do-It-Yourself Lobotomy helps you let go of what you know, what's holding you back from finding better ideas.

How the Do-It-Yourself Lobotomy Works

The Do-It-Yourself Lobotomy tools help refract linear thinking to give you a full spectrum of possibilities and much more colorful ideas (pun painfully noted).

workshop, the ongoing laboratory where I work, is the basis for this book, whose purpose is to bring this "lobotomizing" method to the legions of businesspeople looking for an edge in their professions, an edge created by opening their minds to new, bigger, better ideas to drive the companies they work for.

> *The sharp edge of creativity cuts both ways. It means putting yourself out there on the frontier. It means you could be wrong. You could fail.*

Creative thinking is the only way to make anything better, but its potential pitfalls make it a place where few people have the courage to go as far as they can go.

THE CREATIVE DIRECTOR FOR THE REST OF US

After a successful career as an advertising agency creative director, I left that idea-intensive business to become "creative director for the

I worked in advertising for 20 years before I became a creative thinking coach. I won many awards of which I am very proud. However, the honor that made my parents most proud came in 1990 when I became the youngest person featured in the *Wall Street Journal*'s long-running creative leaders campaign.

rest of us," to paraphrase the introduction of the Apple Macintosh as "the computer for the rest of us."

Having worked with some very smart people in corporate America, in companies such as Colgate-Palmolive, IBM, Gerber, Lotus, Keds, Polaroid, and Hewlett-Packard among many others, I noticed how paralyzed even the brightest people often were when it came to coming up with new ideas on demand. In the ad business I was used to maintaining an environment that helped my people generate hundreds of new ideas by next Thursday's deadline, but I saw the people in the corporate trenches too often struggle to find a few new ideas by next November. That's when I first got the notion to go into the business of helping corporate types open their minds. I've since found the methods in this book not only help stifled businesspeople but are effective thought stimulants for anyone looking for new ideas.

I'd made a career of studying what it takes to get people to come up with fresh, original ideas on demand. For 15 years I led a small ad agency in Providence, Rhode Island, to the pinnacle of this idea-rich business. In the 1980s I taught at the university level as well as for advertising professional organizations. In the 1990s I lectured on creative thinking for the two principal trade publications, *Adweek* and *AdAge*, as well as for the *Wall Street Journal* and over 50 local and regional professional business organizations in the United States and abroad. And I wrote on the topic of creativity for one of the leading publications in the field, *Communication Arts*.

In the early 1990s I made a career shift into an emerging field in which I foresaw a great need—creative coaching. I left my job as president and executive creative director of my ad agency, Leonard/Monahan, to start Before & After, Inc.™, a company dedicated to helping people in business grow creatively. In the ensuing years I have worked for an impressive list of companies, among them Ralston Purina, Compaq, 3M, McDonald's, Southwest Airlines, Viacom, and many others. My workshops have taken me from Hong Kong to Iceland and many points in between. One thing that has become very clear to me is that creativity, both the term and the concept, has come out of the corporate closet. My first business cards read "Creative thinking and problem solving," because I sensed a reluctance on the part of clients and prospects to embrace the term *creativity*. Today the cards read "creativity in business," because more and more leaders at more and more companies see the need for fresh thinking to keep pace in today's fast-changing, dynamic business climate. The concept of "creativity in business" may still be viewed as an oxymoron, but it's out in the open.

> *Today, creativity, as a codified process and conscious skill set, is nearly as high on the corporate agenda as "Total Quality" was during that movement's emerging years.*

ADS BACKWARD

Originally, I set out to bring the secrets of creativity on demand from the ad business to the general business world, and I did just that, working with major companies in non-advertising-related areas right out of the gate. In the past few years, however, I have found that more and more advertising practitioners and the companies they work for have been using my company's services. Lately, it seems that the advertising business is being pressed to be more creative two basic ways, one from within the industry and one from outside. Inside, this historically competitive business has become even more competitive. The industry is undergoing greater change than at any time since the advent of the TV era. The beliefs and skills that carried the most successful people for years are being replaced by the ability to embrace new media options, new marketing paradigms, and a whole new client mind-set. David Lubars, president of Fallon McElligott, says that one of his top priorities is helping his people recognize the new challenges of the ad business to bring greater understanding and value to their clients.

The forces outside the advertising business are just as dramatic. The business planning horizon is no longer measured year to year, and in many companies even quarter to quarter planning is too long term. Technology is allowing the leading companies to be more nimble and helping the followers to keep pace. Strategies that put companies on top of the heap, like Dell's "built to order" model, are knocked off overnight, and competitive edges become dull quicker than the safety razors at an army boot camp.

To those reading this book who are not in the advertising business, know that you will benefit greatly from my in-depth experience in this blisteringly fast-paced business sector whose principal product is ideas.

For those reading this book who *are* in the heat of the advertising industry, know that my forays into literally dozens of other business sectors over the past decade have given me insights into the creative process that can be leveraged in your idea-intensive business in a big way every day.

SHARP TOOLS WITH STRONG HANDLES

The secret to the professional development process in this book is the tools. Through years of exploration and experimentation I have developed a number of creative thinking processes—Do-It-Yourself Lobotomy tools—that over 100,000 people have found to be extremely effective in helping them short-circuit their default mode of traditional thinking. These tools enable people to quickly and easily come up with fresh, exciting ideas whenever they need to. The tools are simple to learn and easy to use, partly because of their memorable, descriptive names, such as 100 MPH Thinking, 180° Thinking, Intergalactic Thinking, and Ask a Better Question.

THE INDISPUTABLE SHIFT TOWARD CREATIVE THINKING

Einstein said, "Imagination is more important than knowledge." This statement has never been more true. High technology is taking away so many left-brain tasks (toll takers, bank tellers, data analysts, etc.) in the same way low technology took away the heavy lifting at the start of the industrial revolution. Economist and investment advisor Harry Dent, in his best-seller *The Roaring 2000s*, says that today's big winners will be those getting the most out of their right brains. Are you as ready as you need to be for this revolution?

> *The information age is now the imagination age.*

Over the centuries, selling ideas as a livelihood was the domain of only a very few. The currency of our great-grandparents and the generations that preceded them was sweat. The industrial revolution took away most of the heavy physical labor. Our parents' generation began more and more to make their livings with their minds instead of their bodies. They *thought* for a living instead of doing the no-brainer work that put food on their parents' tables. It was a dramatic shift in how people earned a living—their professional worth measured in brain power.

Fast-forward to the twenty-first century: Knowledge alone is simply not the edge it used to be in business. The most valuable currency

Creative thinking has never been more valued.

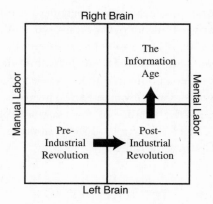

The dramatic shift in how we have earned our livelihoods.
The Information Age is now the Imagination Age.

©2001 Before & After, Inc.

in today's more mature wave of the information age is new ideas. With the present incredible rate of change and the corresponding need to keep pace, the only way to be a true leader is with "constant innovation," as Tom Peters often says. The premium for quick, original thinking has never been greater.

The Ugly Side of the Information Age

The mental gridlock we often experience today that blocks creativity is a result of the cumulative effects of a world that has never been more highly educated and of overdosing on data in the information age.

> *The human mind is capable of infinite imaginary thought, as proven daily by our children. But kids have an advantage over most adults: Their minds aren't filled with knowledge.*

When you know the answer, your mind stops working; when you don't know, your mind tries to fill in the blanks and make it up. The secret to succeeding in business today, to finding more, bigger, better ideas to drive corporate success, isn't simply having more of the same old ideas but in having new ideas. And the secret to having new ideas isn't simply to will it: "I will have a new idea." It is just not that easy.

The secret to getting your mind to embrace a totally fresh, totally precept-shattering idea is to let go of what you know. Because when you *know*, well . . . you *know*. End of story. But when you *don't* know, you wonder what the answer is. The best thinkers of all time have been great wonderers. The greatest strides in the corporate world have come not from *willing* a new idea, but from *wondering* about something better. When you wonder—when you truly let your imagination flow into a state of all possibilities—that is when wonderful things happen.

Wonder leads to wonderful things.

Welcome to [Your Name Goes Here] in Wonderland

Wonder is a simple, childlike state of mind, but is often difficult for many people to achieve.

The problem is that as we know more and more, we need to imagine less, and the center of wonder between our ears gets less and less of a workout. For many people, that part of the brain becomes virtually atrophied. Add to that the incredible fear that is gripping people in business today, the fear of doing or saying something wrong and being passed over or even let go, and there is very little incentive for even trying to think of new ideas.

It's a sad state of affairs. Because certainly the incentive for having new ideas is accomplishment, even greatness. Since the beginning of time the highest achievers have been willing to stick their necks out, along with their minds, to push toward forward-thinking ideas. The great irony is that, although the rate of change and the need for a constant flow of new ideas has never been greater, no generation before us has ever been so reluctant to change. Why? Because no previous generation has been so well educated, had their heads filled with so much knowledge, been so *attached to what they know*, and yet needed so badly *to let go of what they know*.

Although many of the scared working stiffs of our generation are trying to figure out the incentive for fresh thinking, they're being frowned on by management for their risk aversion and "stuckness" in old ways of thinking.

THE BEST MANAGERS WANT FRESH THINKING

Weekly, I hear top managers lamenting the quality of creative thinking they are getting from their people and the lack of inspired thinking they're seeing in the pool of potential employees.

Happily for people like yourself who are reading this book, you'll soon discover a way to let go of what you know whenever you want to — to ramp up your creative thinking ability, to make your mind a nimble, prolific creative idea generator — to give yourself a wealth of the new currency that is driving business today like never before: fresh ideas.

So sit back and enjoy the process of opening up your mind. Embrace your Do-It-Yourself Lobotomy with open arms and an even more open mind. When you've finished this book you'll have the insights and improved skills to be a better thinker than ever before. You'll be the master of a nimble, fertile mind — not just a mind filled with knowledge, but with the ability and willingness to generate fresh, new ideas that will become tomorrow's knowledge.

Your mind is the most powerful tool you'll ever possess. Challenge it. Train it. Use it to propel your career and the fortunes of the companies you work for. Now is your opportunity. Seize it with vigor. And prosper.

Cheat Notes for Introduction

- *Radical technology shifts have resulted in fewer and fewer people working with their bodies and more and more people working with their minds.*

- *Today, knowledge is not as powerful as it used to be; the power today goes to those who can act on the knowledge quickly to get an edge with new ideas.*

- *Creative thinking is the only way to make anything better, but because of its potential pitfalls it's a place few people have the courage to go as far as they can go.*

- *Creative thinking is something high-accomplishing people at leading companies do constantly, because there is always opportunity for improvement.*

- *The ultimate secret to getting your mind to embrace a totally fresh, totally precept-shattering idea is to let go of what you know. In other words, perform a Do-It-Yourself Lobotomy.*

How This Book Works

This book is like the side of the brain you're trying to develop:

random,

chaotic,   **unp-
                                                                          redictable,**

o p e n   t o   a n y t h i n g .

(Or skip this chapter and prove my point.)

I'd like to explain how this book is organized, or unorganized, as the case may be. But first let's talk about why it's organized(?) the way it is.

I believe there is a fair amount of method to coming up with original ideas on demand. That *is* the heart and soul of this book, right?

But I'll also admit ideas *can* come and *do* come without any procedure or inducement. In fact, that is how the creative process works on a great many days. The good days. The easy days. And on those days we can thank the gods of creativity for their generosity. But in business, of course, we don't often have the luxury to wait for that divine inspiration.

> *Over the years, I've found that the best kind of thinking for generating original thought is quite irregular, haphazard, nonlinear, and often illogical.*

To that end, those are the kinds of thought processes that the thinking tools I've developed will bring out.

THE PROCESS TO THE CHAOS

There's some semblance of order to learning the tools covered in this book and the concepts behind the tools. It's an order that will help you grasp them and use them more readily. This book covers some foundational elements first, in Parts I and II primarily, before we get into the tools themselves in Part III. We save what I cleverly categorize as "Dimensionalizing Your New Creative Tools" for Part IV.

As valuable as this order of presentation has been for the more than 100,000 people I've trained over the years (fundamentals of creativity, followed by Do-It-Yourself Lobotomy tools, Ask a Better Question, etc.), I must admit that it's far from perfect. I mean, how can anything related to creativity ever be perfect?

DIFFERENT PEOPLE PROCESS INFORMATION DIFFERENTLY

In my reading of business theory and professional development books over the years, I've often found myself skipping this section or that, jumping around from B to Z and A to L, rereading something I had covered earlier, and so on. I have done this in order to take in the information as I needed it at the various times I picked up the book, with all due respect to how the author intended it to be read.

I have often wondered whether others read (or should I say "process information") in this random, custom-tailored way. It isn't always a strict reading of a book—sometimes it's scanning or rescanning, being reminded by headlines, subheads, and illustrations, or going back to charts or diagrams for reference. It's also using the index as a site map, or skipping ahead to the information you need more urgently, or even reinventing the book in your own form sticking notes in pages, tearing out or copying pages, sticking related articles in the gutter, and so on.

Before writing this book, I did a little "granny survey" of a couple of dozen friends and acquaintances to see how they read professional development books. And guess what? I'm not alone in my reading(?) habits.

THIRD THINGS FIRST

It's becoming increasingly apparent that people today don't necessarily take in information linearly, as many who present it have thought for so long. Whether in books, periodicals, theater, film, songs, TV, advertising, even spoken language, we have all been taught that to communicate clearly we need to state our case in a basic order. Our communications typically have a beginning, a middle, and an end. A case is often presented in brief, the details are given, an analysis or argument is presented based on the facts, and then a conclusion is reached. At least, that was what was practiced for centuries.

Now we're finding out that people don't need or necessarily want an order in the communications thrown at them. They want access to all of the elements, to be sure, but they want to navigate the data *their* way. In this hurry-up world we live and work in, where to-do lists are longer and longer and attention spans are shorter and shorter, people don't want the big five-course feast of information; they want to reach and grasp from the information buffet when and how they please. Witness channel surfing, web browsing, and radio button pushing as evidence of this information consumption behavior.

Consumers of information also want it in smaller, more easily digested portions, as indicated by the layout and portion size of the *Wall Street Journal* front page, *People* magazine articles, CNBC's news sampler, and innumerable other communications vehicles of our time.

"I'LL READ IT MY WAY"

Exhibit A in this argument is how people find their way around an individual web site. If you have access to the "back room" of a web site, look at a detailed web report. Check out the section on "top paths through the site" or whatever they call it in your web report.

Here's what you'll learn: With the vast number of visitors to a web site, even the most frequently chosen routes are used by only a very small percentage of people. What does that tell you? That, given the choice, people say, "Thanks anyway to how you wanted me to navigate this information. I'll find my own way."

So, where am I going with this? Well, this book is not a web site, I'll grant you that. But it is not one of my seminars, either, where I have no choice but to bring everyone through the material in the same order and at the same pace.

Taking your thinking to a higher level.

The School Sisters of Notre Dame are dedicated to education and believe the idle mind is the devil's workshop. So they have vowed to keep their minds active. When not doing their educational work or worshiping, many of the good sisters play games, do puzzles, follow current events and such.

A number of years ago this group came to the attention of the medical science world, as they were outliving the general population and showing fewer signs of Alzheimer's and other forms of dementia. A study was begun to monitor their living habits, and upon their deaths many have been donating their brains to science. Some very interesting discoveries have been made. One such revelation is that many of the sisters do in fact have Alzheimer's. But because of their diverse and dynamic mental activity, it is believed, they have greater healthy resources in other areas of the brain to often take over for some of the performance when the weakened portions lose functionality with age.

Although what researchers call "the Nun Study" represents the largest brain donor population in history, this phenomenon is not unique to this group. But the community's closed population and unique commitment to education makes for interesting study. As of this writing, 678 Sisters are participating.

Many close to this phenomenon agree that an active mind throughout one's life puts the individual in a better position to "manage" the onset of mental aging, so that, when certain neurological pathways begin to dry up (neurons, dendrites, synapses, etc.), other healthier pathways can often assume their work.

The conclusion for the context of this book is that diverse mental activity is not just a way to come up with ideas and solve the problem du jour. It is also a good strategy to ensure that your brain maintains peak performance in general.

If you'd like to learn more on this fascinating topic, enter "Nun Study" into a search engine and find a comfortable chair.

A Book You Don't Have to "Read"

I have built a number of self-navigation elements into this book (as though you weren't going to do just as you pleased anyway). It started with the Creative IQ test you probably just took. After taking this quick little quiz, the order of the chapters in this book has already changed—from a priority perspective, at least. (You already may have read half of this book. See what I mean?)

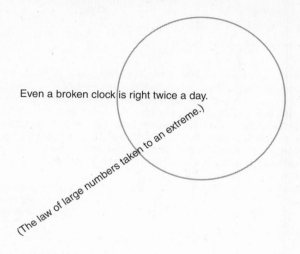

Even a broken clock is right twice a day.

(The law of large numbers taken to an extreme.)

Wooo: This book will have lots of random, out-of-place
material, kind of like this. See more on the law of large
numbers in Chapter 7, page 91.

Following are some of the features that will allow you, even encourage you, to break the rules of thinking even as you (1) read, (2) peruse, (3) scan this book taking in call outs, sidebars and illustrations.

Henceforth you'll find the running text frequently interrupted by what I officially call "Wooo" (Wisdom out of order) elements, where information is presented more randomly, often more graphically, easy to read, sometimes totally out of the blue. These Wooo elements provide some balance to the running text by addressing the other side of your brain—the less structured, more free-flowing part that this book is helping you master.

Although it is my objective (and my private, perverted pleasure) to surprise you quite often with these free-style elements, there is sometimes some structure to help you take advantage of the lack of structure. Here are some of the elements to watch for.

Wooo!

These "Wisdom out of order" elements themselves consist of little blurbs, quotes, mini–case histories, and illustrations that may or may not have anything to do with the section where they're found. Some of these Wooo elements direct you to specific pages where the topic is covered in more detail.

> ### The Lobotomy Files
>
> Blah blah blah blah, blah blah blah, blah blah blah blah blah blah blah blah blah blah blah blah blah blah blah. Blah, blah blah blah blah blah blah blah, blah blahblah blah blah blah blah blah blah blah. Blah blah, blah blah blah blah blah blah blah blah. Blah, blah blah blah blah blah blah, blah blahblah blah blah blah blah. Blah blah, blah blah blah blah blah blah blah blah. Blah, blah blah blah blah blah blah blah, blah blahblah blah blah blah blah blah blah blah. Blah blah, blah blah blah blah blah blah blah blah.
>
> Jane Doe
> XYZ Company

This is what a Lobotomy File looks like, only the
text is a bit more meaningful.

A Wooo may actually have something to do with the section you're reading at that point in time but relate more closely to another section. Then again, it may have almost nothing to do with the matter at hand or even contradict it. Fine. It's there to make you think and give you a quick path to where this tidbit is covered in greater detail.

Cheat Notes

Another element I've incorporated to help you process the information more organically is what I call "cheat notes." At the end of each section is a quick distillation of most of the major points made in that section. These cheat notes have a few purposes:

1. When read immediately after you finish each chapter, they help you recap what you've just read.
2. If you choose to skim some or all of the book in advance of reading, you can use them to take a quick peek into the content of each chapter.
3. Cheat notes are also an excellent way to review the book at a later time, long after you've read it, using the triggers to help you navigate to sections you may wish to read again.

The Lobotomy Files

Sprinkled throughout the book are statements from real people who have undergone our Do-It-Yourself Lobotomy (mini–case histories, if you will). Many have experienced this psychic operation some time ago and have been reaping the benefits for years. Some of these people have chosen to remain anonymous, but I can assure you the statements are theirs.

Gaining the fullest results from your Do-It-Yourself Lobotomy (DIYL) will require a commitment on your part to change the way you think. This takes effort and discipline. And, similar to testimonials in diet or fitness books laden with real-world transformations, actual statements from happy DIYL victims give you encouragement in your changeover to a more original, prolific idea generator.

In the spirit of Wooo, many of these Lobotomy files are totally random and may have little to do with the chapter in which they appear, but they might steer you toward related reading elsewhere.

The Rewards of a Great Idea

> *When you have a great idea you have something that has tremendous potential. Like an asteroid crashing into the ocean, it can cause monumental initial impact and can effect a tidal wave of repercussions for amazing distances for a very long time.*

Someone had the idea of the wheel. That tidal wave is still cresting and causing impact today.

Of course, not all ideas are quite so magnificent or recognized as world-changing events. Take that simple little fastener device called the button. Who had that idea? I don't know, but that concept has surely had a great, long-lasting impact on almost everyone on this planet. I bet that if I counted the wheels and buttons in my life I would find that the button plays as important a role (keeping my pants up) as the wheel (getting me to the airport).

When you come up with a new idea, big or small, think about its potential long-term effect. In the thinking/doing equation covered in Chapter 18, "Mind Farming™," I talk about how most of what we do in the course of a day (in meetings, on the phone, at the computer, traveling, etc.) is in the service of executing an idea.

How good is that idea? Will it have a positive, lasting impact? Will it blast through the atmosphere and fizzle before splashdown? Will it change things affirmatively and irrevocably?

A great idea can make a company—Xerox, 3M, Volkswagen. It can make an industry—computers, automobiles, aerospace. It can

The birth of an idea:

In the grand scheme of things, that magical flash of brilliance doesn't take long. What? A second? Maybe two?

The time it takes to execute an idea:

Again, in the grand scheme of things, it doesn't take a great deal of time to execute an idea, either. At least not that long compared to the ongoing life of an idea.

The ongoing life of a great idea (definitely indefinite):

This is a whole different story. There's the original idea in its fundamental form. Then there's the various permutations of the original idea during its early phases, often just minor modifications of the core idea. And then there are the subsequent generations of the idea that might look and feel quite different from the granddaddy, but would not be in existence without it.

Timeline of a great idea

make a career — Steve Jobs, Herb Kelleher, Sam Walton. Of course, some careers spawn companies and industries. (Or is it the other way around?)

Wow! All because of an idea? A computer that's easy to use. An airline that's inexpensive. A store that sells virtually the same things everyone else sells, but is defined by customer service.

Of course, not all great ideas live forever. Actually, a good many of them enjoy an even greater afterlife when they finally do die. An afterlife in the form of subsequent generations of ideas that would not have been born if not for the "genetic coding" of the original idea. For example, an idea like rockabilly is totally overshadowed by its offspring, rock 'n' roll.

There's also the afterlife where an idea lives on not because it is still viable, but because it is recognized as having made a big impact in its time — an idea like the great pyramids of Egypt. Although in some cases the idea is long since deceased, its spirit may live on and inspire others to come up with equally grand ideas totally unrelated to this now dead but revered concept.

Even the lasting ideas are not all huge, industry-breeding, direction-changing concepts. One idea that comes to mind from a project I was involved with early on in my marketing career is the universal orthotic insert we see in so many shoes these days. This idea emerged from the mind of a very creative podiatrist, Dr. Rob Roy McGregor, who designed the first running shoe developed under the Etonic brand during the 1970s running boom. Initially called the "single-unit heel and arch support," this device adapted the concept of the orthotic, an individually prescribed rigid device worn in shoes to correct pronation and foster proper heel plant, and turned it into a universal performance mechanism that is in virtually all quality athletic footwear today, as well as in many nonathletic shoes. A big idea that changed things, possibly forever, if only in a narrow, underappreciated area, Dr. McGregor's concept proved to be immortal.

Even if immortality is not your goal, you must be mindful that an idea has a life and an afterlife. A great idea can continue to deliver value for years beyond its initial inception. Whether or not you personally reap all of the rewards of this idea, you must know that you have created a living thing that will have an impact, help others, maybe generate income and livelihoods for generations to come. That is a great reward. And a great responsibility. Which leads us to the other side of this coin, which isn't always as bright and shiny.

Timeline of a great idea (continued)

Energizer™ Bunny used with permission and acknowledgment that this is a great, enduring advertising idea.

The Consequences of a Bad Idea

It has often been said that a bad idea is like a virus. It lives. It grows. It sustains. It spreads.

When you execute a bad idea it can be like taking the lid off that potent alien virus vial; once it's out, there's little hope for those who come in contact with it.

> *Bad ideas can spread even faster than good ideas. Their ramifications to the people involved can spread even faster in the ultracompetitive corporate world, where the grapevine often makes the news services look like the pony express.*

Does the saying, "Distance yourself from the stench," sound familiar? No longer is the problem the thing that smells; it's the stink left behind that is the problem.

As for all those philosophers who say, "There's no such thing as a bad idea," I invite them to see how long they can stick around without holding their noses when some of these whoppers hit the fan.

Elsewhere in this book I talk about the fact that a bad idea—even one that's as bad as bad can be—cannot hurt anyone, that is, until it is executed. Well, in this section we're talking about executing bad ideas, not just thinking of them.

A bad idea can derail the best-laid plans of any group. It can put a good company out of business. It can take away people's jobs, cause empires to fall, and cost a lot of people a ton of money.

The birth of an idea:

In the grand scheme of things, that magical flash of brilliance (?) doesn't take long. What? A second? Maybe two?

The time it takes to execute an idea:

Again, in the general scheme of things, it doesn't take a lot of time to execute an idea, good or bad.

At least not that long compared to the ongoing life of any kind of idea.

The ongoing life of a "bad" idea (can you possibly get your mind around the concept of eternity?):

This is a whole different story. There's the idea itself in whatever form. Then there's the baggage that goes along with the bad idea. The questions. The second-guessing. The echoes of ghosts past. With truly bad ideas the public can have a very long and vivid memory. And your boss's memory can be even longer and stronger.

Timeline of a lousy idea

Of course, a good idea, poorly executed, can also do a lot of damage. And a bad idea that's well executed can . . . no, I don't think so. Basically, if we can have both good ideas and good execution, why would we ever settle for bad ideas or bad execution?

The good thing about bad ideas is that they so often put themselves out of their own misery. Die, bad idea. Die.

So, no harm done, right?

Wrong.

Exhibit A: the Edsel.

Yes, the product died (and perhaps not soon enough). But the idea of the Edsel lives on. That's the whole point here.

Because even if the idea dies or you're smart enough to kill it yourself, the aftermath of "Whose idea was it, anyway?" can linger on indefinitely.

> *Similarly to the timeline of a great idea, a bad idea, while taking relatively little time to conceive and execute, can have ramifications for years and years and years.*

Consider an "ouch" followed by an "ouch" and so on and so on to the *n*th degree.

Timeline of a lousy idea (continued)

Can you possibly comprehend
the concept of eternity?

The First Real Chapter (Finally!)

Yes, you are creative!

Have you ever had an idea? Sure you have.

Have you ever solved a problem? Absolutely. Probably a few today.

So you have the ability to come up with ideas and solve problems. Great. Now, answer this question: Do you get the idea that you're looking for every time? Do you get the solution to your problem every time? When you need it? With little effort or pain?

That's why you're reading this book. It's not that you don't have creative capability; everyone has infinite creative capacity. I mean, just remember when you were a kid . . . you lived in your imagination almost 100 percent of the time. It's not that you don't possess creativeness. It's that you have an inconsistency in accessing it, a discrepancy in coming up with big ideas when you need them. That's what this book will help you do. This book will help you become a more conscious, therefore more consistent, creative thinker.

A PLANET OF UNCONSCIOUS THINKERS

What do you do on your best days, when you have a great idea? If you knew, wouldn't you do it all the time to improve your hit rate?

Is it something that you *don't* do on those days when you have a great idea? Are you at all aware of what you don't do on those good days?

Is it what you don't do on the bad days? Perhaps it's what you *do* on the bad days that's getting in the way.

If you're not particularly conscious of your creative thinking abilities, you're not a freak. Most people aren't very aware when it comes to thinking. Most people simply don't think about how they think.

We all have good days; we all have bad days. The good days feel so good. "Yes!" "A great idea!" "A solution to a problem!" There's nothing quite like it.

And then there are the bad days. "Oh no, it's not coming." "Oh, this isn't any good." Or worse yet, sometimes it feels like a great idea—"Yes!" And a few days later. . . . "What was I thinking?"

We're so inexact.

Why the inconsistency? Because, for the most part, we're unaware of what we do when we come up with great ideas, and we're unaware of what we do when we don't come up with great ideas or when we come up with less-than-great or even absolutely horrible ideas. We're simply unconscious thinkers.

PRACTICE DOESN'T MAKE PERFECT

> *I have a golf pro, a guy who really likes challenges, who says, "Practice doesn't make perfect. Only perfect practice makes perfect."*

I don't know about you, but when I'm on the golf range—supposedly practicing—I'm usually just swinging away, totally unconscious of what I'm doing, getting really consistent at being inconsistent.

Did you learn the right way to think when you were about four months old? That's when we first started to formulate our own thoughts. Don't tell me you've been practicing imperfectly all these years! No wonder so many of your ideas wind up in the rough.

Well, guess what? You don't have as much to learn from scratch about creative thinking and problem solving as you might think. You see, this book isn't going to teach you as much as it's going to help you recognize what you do on your best days.

Recognizing, not learning. See? Already it's easier than you thought.

Have you ever practiced Intergalactic Thinking? Sure you have. You just don't know it.

How about 180° Thinking? Have you ever engaged in that type of thinking? Guess what? You've done that, too. Probably hundreds of times. You're just not aware.

Have you ever tried 100 MPH Thinking? Again, sure you have. You've been practicing all of these types of thinking processes for years. But, I hate to tell you, you've likely been practicing imperfectly because you have been practicing unconsciously.

Intergalactic Thinking, 180° Thinking, and 100 MPH Thinking are some of the thinking methods we cover in this book. I didn't make up these thinking techniques. They have been used by high-achieving people for centuries. And, yes, you've used them on your best days. I just made up the names—handles, if you will—to help people better grasp these valuable tools and to make them easier to use.

CODIFYING THE CREATIVE PROCESS

As a creative thinking coach, I work with people in industry in two principal ways. I help people improve their creative thinking abilities in a general sense through corporate training and skills development sessions. I also facilitate high-output brainstorming sessions geared to specific issues, challenges, and opportunities (new product ideas, promotional ideas, naming products, etc.).

One of my most active industry sectors is advertising, a field in which creativity is so codified that companies actually have a "creative brief," a "creative department," and *creative* is often used as a noun to describe the advertising itself, as in, "The creative looks great!" Frankly, I understand creative thinking much better than most people do. I understand creative thinking in a way that can help you become more conscious, consistent thinkers.

Now, being unconscious about creativity hasn't made you totally ineffective. Hardly. But you could be better if you were more conscious. Let me explain with an illustration in an entirely different area.

SIT DOWN FOR THIS

Let's talk about sitting. Are you a conscious sitter? Maybe you're sitting properly now. Maybe you have the right posture quite often. Maybe not. But do you know how to do it right? Are you a conscious sitter? I'm a conscious sitter.

A number of years ago I had a problem with my back. I went to see a chiropractor and he told me I was sitting wrong. I was having pain and he helped me make a few minor adjustments in my posture and the pain went away. I'm now a conscious sitter. And, for the most part, the pain is gone. Oh sure, on occasion I forget and I slip back into my old habits. But because I am now more conscious, I can remind myself and I can relieve the pain. I make minor adjustments and I don't have the pain.

This book is designed to make you a more conscious thinker so you can make minor adjustments to improve your game substantially. These little adjustments will improve your ability to come up with big ideas, improve your ability to solve problems, and do it all with great consistency.

Unconscious sitter.   Conscious sitter.

A DO-IT-YOURSELF LOBOTOMY INCISION GOES HERE

What you know hurts you.

> *Virtually all of the thoughts that you process daily are conspiring to make you a boring, uninspired thinker.*

Scientists tell us that we have billions of thoughts running through our minds every day. On a conscious level, it's estimated that we process between 125 and 130 bits of data every second. That's over 11 million bits of data—just on the *conscious* level—each day.

Then there are the subconscious and superconscious levels. Literally billions of bits of data on or near the surface of our minds.

Think of your first-grade teacher. How long did it take to access that data? We each possess a veritable supercomputer between our ears.

⋆⊹⋆

HOW THE MIND WORKS (KIND OF)

Each of these stars represents a bit of data. Each of us lives in our own galaxy of thought, where our mind resides almost all of the time because our thoughts default to the known. My own galaxy includes thoughts of family, my environment, my favorite sports teams, and so on.

Where New Ideas Are Found

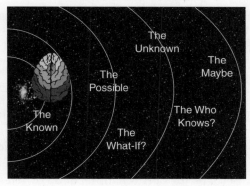

New ideas don't reside in our known. Solutions to problems that are unsolved at the present are not part of our home galaxy of thought. Einstein said, "You cannot solve a problem using what got you there." Staying in the known, which is our natural state of mind, prevents us from exploring other possibilities.

How New Ideas Are Found

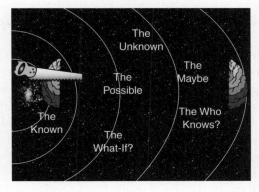

The Do-It-Yourself Lobotomy will help you let go of what you know, even if for just a nanosecond, to help your mind wander. Because when you know, you know—end of story. But when you don't know, you wonder—and your mind wanders—and that's when wonderful things happen.

❖

Sadly, for most of us, the vast majority of the data we process is old data. Old, stale thoughts we and others have had many, many times before.

> 95% of what you think today, you thought yesterday.
>
> Deepak Chopra

Actually, thinking in the *known* is our best friend most of the time, but it's our worst enemy when it's time to come up with new ideas. New ideas don't happen in the known. They happen in the *unknown,* the maybe, the what-if.

This book will help you disengage your imagination from your rational mind to free you up for greater creative thought. To let go of what you know, perhaps for only a nanosecond. To release your mind to entertain a new idea. To wonder.

You can look at it sort of as a lobotomy of the Do-It-Yourself variety. The process is painless and easy. All it requires is a little open-mindedness, so to speak.

THE MIND OF A CHILD

We human beings are by nature very creative creatures. Just look at any child. Look at how you were as a kid. Wasn't your imagination quite active and fertile?

Then you learned things. You filled your mind with facts, data, information, knowledge. All good things to help you grow and function in the many aspects of your life: work, play, family, and so forth.

For generations before us it's been pretty much the same: You experience life; you fill the mind with data. For those of us walking erect on this planet today, this mind cramming no longer just happens in the course of living; it's now drilled into our heads in our formal education, in the expectations of our parents and other influential people. We're bombarded by data, data, data, knowledge, knowledge, knowledge. In this information age, knowledge is no longer an edge; it's expected. Everyone has it. Everyone has to have it to play the game.

> *But there's a double edge to this mighty thinking sword. The more you know, the less you have to imagine. And the less you imagine, the more routine your thoughts become.*

Let this book help you let go of what you know just long enough to discover something better.

As a creativity coach in business, I discovered years ago the key to helping people think more creatively.

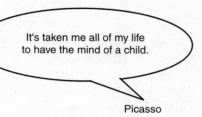

It's taken me all of my life to have the mind of a child.

Picasso

The secret isn't to will new ideas; it's to let go of what you know.

Think about that. Letting go of what you know so you can better use the vast resources of your mind. Simple? Yes. Easy? Well, yes again—that is, if you gain some very basic insights into the thought process and use a little discipline to master some new thinking habits.

GOOD IDEAS GET IN THE WAY OF GREAT IDEAS

It is my experience working with people in business that many people suffer from the same tragic flaw in their creative process. We don't come up with great ideas because we come up with good ideas. And, yes, as you might guess, the vast majority of these good ideas are ideas we already know.

Good is the enemy of great.

Voltaire

A HEAD TALKS ABOUT STAYING FRESH

In an article in *Time Out New York* in May 2001, David Byrne, former Talking Heads front man and all-around creative genius, discussed the challenges of staying fresh in an area where you have deep experience and familiarity. "You cannot unlearn what you know and go back to square one, so I try to put myself in a situation where I'm off balance. Then I have to struggle and scrape a bit rather than fall back on what I already know."

It's not just a matter of going beyond what we know without effort or thought. If it were only that easy, we'd all do it.

The part that takes no effort is the part you already do too well: rational thought, staying in the known.

Don't think you've been doing it wrong all these years. This is the way the brain works. Known data is the raw material for rational thought. But you need to go beyond rational thought to be a consistently creative thinker.

> If we want to solve a problem that we have never solved before, we must leave the door to the unknown ajar.
>
> Richard P. Feynman
> 20th-century U.S. physicist

The following chapters are an armchair version of the acclaimed creativity workshop that my associates and I conduct for thousands of people in hundreds of companies in scores of industries annually. The workshop is called The Do-It-Yourself Lobotomy. It's a proven method based on a few basic insights and the use of a few simple creative thinking power tools. We've used this method to help airlines find new and better ways to make their passengers more comfortable. We've used it to help a major computer company perform better phone support. We've used it with dozens of advertising agencies to help them create better advertisements and find new business-building ideas quicker. We've helped the world's largest snack maker explore new tasty treats. We've used it to help one of the world's largest computer textbook companies bring better learning to children.

The Do-It-Yourself Lobotomy works. Heck, you've been doing it for years. On your best days, that is.

Don't tell me you've been unconscious about it.

⟡

BE A TIGER

A very good friend of mine, Richard Wilde, who understands creativity like few people on this planet, tells a funny story about how adults so often lose touch with the imaginative child within.

A number of years ago he was asked to address his daughter's second grade class. As department head of advertising and design at the School for Visual Arts in New York City, Richard is skilled at designing problems, asking questions, and creating challenges for students to bring out their creativity. Richard gave this roomful of seven-year-olds the following simple assignment: Be a tiger. Immediately, the kids wrinkled their noses, showed their claws, and began growling and pawing the air. Instantly. Effortlessly.

A short time later, Richard gave the same simple assignment to a roomful of his second-year graduate students. "Be a tiger," he told them. The room fell silent. They looked cautiously at one another out of the corners of their eyes. One student asked, "Can we research it?" Another queried, "When is it due?" Yet another asked, "What medium?" Richard just smiled to himself and told them, "Forget it, it's too hard for you," and went on to the next assignment.

❖

Cheat Notes for Chapter 1:
The First Real Chapter

- *Everyone has infinite creative capacity.*

- *The more you know, the less you have to imagine. And the less you imagine, the more routine your thoughts become.*

- *New ideas don't happen in the known. They happen in the unknown, the maybe, the what-if.*

- *Most people don't come up with great ideas because they come up with good ideas, then stop.*

- *You must get out of the deep grooves of rational thought to be a consistent creative thinker.*

- *Little adjustments can improve your ability to come up with big ideas, improve your ability to solve problems, and do so with great consistency.*

PART II

Understanding and Demystifying Creativity

There are some fundamental aspects of creative thinking that are ill understood and even grossly misunderstood by many people. This lack of understanding often severely limits their creative potential.

Some of the more basic precepts are so foundational that not to grasp them imposes a ceiling for creative accomplishment, and worse, can actually be a detriment to achievement.

Forget the creative thinking power tools that'll be covered in the later chapters of this book, your Do-It-Yourself Lobotomy instruments, as it were. Yes, those surefire methods of thinking have been leading great thinkers to big ideas since the beginning of time. But if you can't grasp some of the core concepts behind creativity in this section, then all the effort to learn all of the techniques in the world will be greatly compromised.

> *Basically, to take greatest advantage of the amazing resourcefulness of creativeness, you need to understand creativity at a fundamental level and know its role in your everyday life.*

"Gee, that paycheck looks a little fatter this month."

Timeline of a great idea (continued)

Timeline of a lousy idea (continued)

Creativity = Problem Solving

Do you like problems?

Is this a trick question?

Sure is.

When I ask this question at my seminars, sometimes a few brave souls raise their hands. They understand something of the role of problems in creative thinking. They see the value of problems. Intellectually, that is.

Of course, when people walk into any of their offices with 10 problems, these enlightened souls, too, can find themselves thinking of problems as impediments to accomplishment rather than as booster rockets for creativity.

Problems are a fundamental part of the creative thinking process. Actually, I'll go even further with that claim and state that problems are a fundamental part of accomplishment.

Most people who study creativeness agree that problem solving is essential to creative achievement. Most who truly understand creativeness believe it's virtually impossible to be creative without a problem.

Think about it. To this point in your life you have been at your best, creatively, when you are solving problems. And that's true whether or not you understand fully the role of problems in creative accomplishment.

Look at your resume. Your achievement at every stage of your career is the result of problem solving.

> *Without the daily challenges of problems, what the hell is it that you do, anyway?*

Yes, occasionally you have those good days when no major problems present themselves. Good days? Oh, really? Sorry, but if you have too many of those days, your company may not need you very much longer.

YOUR CAREER HIGHLIGHTS FILM

Problems cause you to stretch, to see how good you really are. Your resume is like an athlete's highlights film. When baseball greats like Derek Jeter or Ken Griffey Jr. are renegotiating their contracts, what do you think their highlights films feature? They put their problem-solving skills front and center. To demonstrate how good they are, do you think they are going to feature a segment where they make a routine play—catching an easy ball hit weakly right at them? I don't think so.

They're going to show themselves stretching deep into "the hole," as baseball people like to call it, or jumping impossibly high to snare a nearly hopeless catch. They are problem solvers; they can stretch to

Some people think the Pentium II is the fastest processor in the world. Not quite. The chip inside every new Power Macintosh G3 is up to twice as fast. Think different.

180° Faster Communication

Apple Computer touted the speed of their (then new) G3 chip with this print ad (and companion TV commercial) that made a very quick, highly effective statement. A conventional way to communicate "our chip is faster" would have been to say, or somehow show, that the G3 chip is faster. Apple, proving that they practice what they preach when they say, "Think different," showed the competition's chip as being slow with this 180° approach. (For more on 180° Thinking, see Chapter 8.)

superhuman limits when they need to. Their highlights films show them going beyond the routine. As does *your* highlights film—that is, your resume.

By definition, accomplishment is problem solving. And it's very nearly impossible to be creative without problems.

Even the fine artist has a problem. It's called the blank canvas. Or the slab of marble. Or the blank page. Or maybe paying the rent is the problem. Even the successful rock star has problems. Maybe it's the last CD. "Can I top it?" "Can I grow creatively?" "Can I pay for that new house with the Olympic-size swimming pool shaped like a guitar?"

❧❀❧

A QUICK DEMONSTRATION OF CREATIVITY = PROBLEM SOLVING

Let me demonstrate how fundamental problem solving is to creativity. Actually, you're going to have to help me demonstrate it. Here's what I'd like you to do.

Ready? Be creative.

That's it. Be creative.

Go ahead. Put the book down if you must. Now be creative.

Come on. What are you waiting for? Be creative, for pity's sake.

Have you done it yet?

Are you ready to give up?

When I do this with people at my seminars, one of two things happens. The thing that happens about 99 percent of the time is nothing. I'll pick on someone in the front row. I'll say, "Please be creative for us." And that poor, pathetic soul just sits there wishing he or she had never sat in the front, wondering what you're supposed to do when asked to "be creative."

See? You're not alone in having a hard time figuring out how to be creative out of the blue. Without a problem, that is. These on-the-spot victims look around for answers, with looks that say, "What am I supposed to do?" "I'll give it a shot." "I'll try to be creative for you." "But just exactly what am I supposed to do?"

Think about it. How can you possibly be creative without a context? And for all intents and purposes that context is a problem.

The other 1 percent of the time when I ask that person in the front row to "please be creative for us," I get the same look of shock, the hesitation, and the self-consciousness. But some people can only handle that awkward silence so long, and these individuals might stand up and make weird faces or wacky gestures or offer up strange sounds like a wounded duck or something. It's not a pretty sight. Basically, that individual created a problem to solve.

A PROBLEM IS A MUST

I believe it's impossible to be creative without a problem. We are all at our creative best when we're solving problems.

A real problem, that is.

You see, many things we call problems really aren't. Let's examine this stuff, *problems*.

When you solve a problem what's the language you usually use? "I *found* a solution to my problem." Or . . . "I *created* a solution."

If you *found* a solution, did you really have a problem? I mean, the answer already existed. You did *find* it, after all.

Here's how this so-called problem-solving soap opera might play out, for example:

"We have to do a holiday promotion to move some merchandise," someone in retail marketing might say. "We have a problem!"

"What did we do last year?" asks the white knight in wing tips.

"Yeah, you're right," admits the alarmist, then adds, "But we'll do it totally differently this year; we'll take new photos, change the type-face—totally different."

This team of bozos didn't have a real problem. They had a misplaced answer to a question they had asked many times before. They knew the answer. It was in the known, so there was no creativity.

Sometimes the drama plays out like this:

"We have to do a holiday promotion. I wasn't here last year. What did you do?"

No, this time it's not in the problem solver's known. It's in someone else's known. But the answer is still found. Therefore it's not a real problem.

If you can't find a solution, if the solution does not already exist, then you have a real problem and you have no choice but to be creative.

That drama sounds like this:

"We didn't have this holiday promotion last year. It's a new holiday. No company has ever done this promotion. I wonder what we could do."

BAM! The wonder gland kicks in. Now you have a *real* problem. Now you are in the creative realm. Not *finding* but *creating*.

The Lobotomy Files

Insuring Competitive Success

If an organization is to move forward and compete effectively today, it must have people with the right attitude. The fast-paced thinking methods of The Do-It-Yourself Lobotomy got the mental juices flowing and stimulated the mighty power of innovation and creativity to help shape dramatic change at The Amica Companies. This is of particular importance to us given the fiercely competitive property/casualty and life insurance marketplaces in which we operate today.

The fundamentals our management team across the country learned from The Do-It-Yourself Lobotomy's interactive and fun-filled thinking approaches, along with strong support and encouragement from our senior executives, has truly energized our organization. Our talented team members are now liberated and exercising the muscles of their minds. Clearly, we now have an organization that has become much more open-minded to opportunity and better equipped to innovate its way to even greater success.

Tom Taylor, President & CEO
The Amica Companies
Lobotomized, along with 180
colleagues, 2000

PROBLEMS DON'T HAVE TO BE TORTURE
(Or Maybe They Should Be)

Many years ago when we were developing a low-budget TV commercial, my creative team partner and I encountered a problem that caused us to stretch to a place that helped us generate a wonderful idea we probably would not have come up with otherwise.

The spot was for a software product whose primary advantage over other software at that time was its extreme ease of use. We looked at many executions, among them an approach that showed or mentioned the problems of "harder-to-learn, harder-to-use" software. (This concept of demonstrating the problem with the competition is one of the more popular uses of 180° Thinking, which you'll learn more about in Chapter 8.) I forget exactly which creative approach we finally took to the animation house; all I remember is that we couldn't afford to do it. This was in the waning days of cell animation, just before computers made this art form almost obsolete and a lot less expensive. And therein was the problem. Since animation costs were $1,000 per second and we had a budget of only $7,000 for the video portion of this commercial, we came up 8 seconds short of our 15-second target.

"Can't we find more money?" we pleaded with the client.

"No."

"Can't we find a way to stretch the budget?" we pleaded with the animation house.

"Well, you *can* afford animation as long as the commercial has no more than seven seconds of unduplicated animation," they said. "So if you can find a creative approach that allows you to loop the frames, like a hummingbird flapping its wings or a flag waving in the breeze, you don't pay for the part that repeats."

Hmm.

We had a problem. Looping the animation cells was a solution. But how could we creatively pull this off? I remember thinking, "This is crazy, we can't let a production reality like this dictate the conceptual direction of the TV spot." Well, before we discounted this approach entirely, my partner and I thought of the Chinese water torture. The whole premise of this ancient, perhaps apocryphal, exercise was the excruciating pain caused by the tedium of the process. Wasn't that the problem inherent in the evil competitor's software product?

Bam! A problem caused us to stretch. No, it wasn't the usual kind of problem you'd expect to prompt fresh thinking. After all, it was just some quirky production value reality. But I have to tell you, I'm not sure we would have come up with this idea, which happened to be right on strategy, if this problem hadn't caused us to think in an arbitrary way.

Footnote: The campaign went on to cause a minor stir in the high-tech marketing world, as it outperformed Microsoft and a dozen other major players in its primary run at Comdex, the technology industry's major trade show.

❖

YOU CAN LOBOTOMIZE

> *When you can't find a solution to a problem, a real problem, because no solution exists, then you have no choice but to be creative.*

Suppose you have seen the problem a hundred times before. Does that mean you can't be creative? Certainly not.

You can choose to *not know* the answer you already have and to wonder what a better answer might be. The most highly realized creative people do this every day. They choose to *wonder.* But for us mere mortals, it's very hard to not know what we know. For many of us it's virtually impossible.

And that's where the Do-It-Yourself Lobotomy comes in.

The Do-It-Yourself Lobotomy thinking tools that comprise the next section of this book are very valuable for helping us think creatively whether or not we know the answer to our current problem. Although these tools *can* and *do* help you find fresh answers to real problems — creating truly new situations when you cannot find a solution in the known — they are particularly valuable when you *know* an answer but are looking for a better one.

All of the tools that I have developed over the years — 100 MPH Thinking, Intergalactic Thinking, 180° Thinking, and others — are designed to help you quickly and effortlessly let go of what you know (i.e., lobotomize yourself) to put you in that state of wonder where wonderful things happen.

All of these tools are ways of turning your so-called problems, those for which you usually *find* tried-and-true solutions, into real problems, the kind that cause you to stretch your imagination. These are the types of problems that help us to be as good as we can be, problems that lead to real accomplishment.

Cheat Notes for Chapter 2:
Creativity = Problem Solving

- It's virtually impossible to be creative without a problem.

- You are at your best creatively when you are solving problems, because problems cause you to stretch, to find out how good you really are.

- If you can't find a solution, if the solution does not already exist, then you have a real problem and you have no choice but to create the solution.

- If a solution does exist, you can choose to not know the answer and simply decide to wonder what a better answer might be, as most highly realized creative people do.

Change Your Thinking about Change

Now I want to talk about a fundamental part of creativity that has been one of the foremost triggers of some of the greatest ideas of all time. In fact, it's probably *the* best impetus for great ideas. Yet it's resisted by people around the world and has been for centuries. I'm talking about change.

In Chapter 2 we talked about problems that cause us to stretch. We showed that creativity and problem solving are virtually the same thing. We also demonstrated that we're usually at our best when solving problems.

Well, think about it: What causes most problems?

That's right, *change.*

Things change. You're in a situation you haven't been in before. You don't have a ready answer. You have a problem. You wonder what

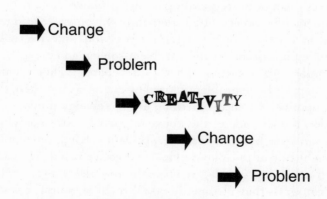

The creative problem-solving cycle.

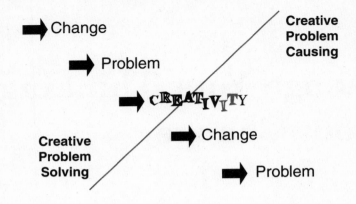

Why be a creative problem solver?
Leaders are creative problem causers.

the answer is. Aha, you have the primary condition for creativity — wonder.

As this diagram of the creative problem-solving cycle points out, change causes problems that trigger creative thinking. And that brings us to a place where creative things happen.

But what does creativity do? Creativity changes things, which causes problems. This triggers the cycle to go on indefinitely. The question is where are you playing in the cycle?

Change is inevitable. It's going to happen or someone's going to make it happen. We all have to play on the creative problem-solving playing field. If you play on the reactive side (the left side of the diagram), where you address change by responding to the problem caused by change (usually effected by others, often competitors), you are forced to be creative, and at least you're playing. And you don't survive in business unless you're playing the creative problem-solving game.

But leaders are proactive. They cause change. They create. They don't just start with the problem caused by change; very often, they provide the initiative to create something new, to change things.

Whereas the left side of the above creative problem-solving cycle, left of the creative burst, is creative problem solving, one could argue that the right side of this playing field is creative problem *causing*. And most high-achieving people, in business and elsewhere, are creative problem causers — they change things. Which, of course, causes problems for the competition.

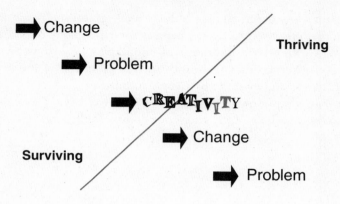

Survive change. Or thrive on change. It's all a
matter of perspective and self-motivation.

Michael Dell changed the rules of how PCs were sold. He caused problems for his competition that took years for them to neutralize.

Herb Kelleher of Southwest Airlines causes problems for competing carriers every time he enters a new market. When Southwest entered my home market of Providence, Rhode Island, they caused many other airlines to change their fare structures, change their routes, and even caused US Airways and Delta to launch subbrands in this market, with MetroJet and Delta Express, respectively.

Oh, sure, when you change things it also causes problems for you, but you're going to be dealing with problems every day of your life; they're the raw material for accomplishment. We discussed that earlier.

> *You can either deal with someone else's problems, or you can deal with problems on your own terms.*

Dell and Southwest set the bar just as high for themselves as they did for the competition. The main difference was that they knew it was coming. They were prepared. It caught the competition flat-footed.

When *you* make the changes, you are leading as opposed to following. According to the old business adage, "If you don't make dust, you eat dust." You can play on either side. In fact, you *must* play on one side or the other. Just to survive, you have to play on the left side. Those who truly play on the right side of this formula are the ones who thrive.

The great irony about change is that it's our greatest ally for accomplishment, yet most people resist change. Some people avoid it like the plague. In working with hundreds of companies in dozens of industries, I have observed that resistance to change is one of the greatest deterrents to accomplishment by people in business.

If you can simply change your mind about change, you can go a long way toward vastly improving your creative thinking.

Boss calls you into his office. And for a change you're not worried.

Timeline of a great idea (continued)

Timeline of a lousy idea (continued)

Cheat Notes for Chapter 3:
Change Your Thinking About Change

- Resistance to change by the vast majority of people in business is one of the greatest deterrents to accomplishment.

- Change is inevitable. It's either going to happen organically or someone's going to make it happen.

- Change causes problems, which trigger creative thinking, which brings about more change.

- You don't survive in business unless you're playing the creative problem-solving game. You don't thrive unless you are effecting change.

- Leaders are proactive. They cause change. They create.

- You can either deal with someone else's problems or you can deal with problems on your own terms.

CHAPTER 4

Creativity versus Talent

Another foundational concept about creativity that is a tremendous misconception for many people concerns the relationship between creativeness and artistic talent. They are not the same. Let's prove it. Look at the two pictures below.

One is an early Dutch portrait. The other is a photograph of an onion ring tree and dip dispenser. I ask you to think carefully about this before you answer: Which is more creative?

It's so easy to look at the wonderful portrait, the product of tremendous artistic talent, and think, "That's where the creativity lies in this matchup," when in fact there's very little if any creativity exhibited there. If this portrait represents what this seventeenth-century gentleman looked like, then the painter didn't create anything. He re-created the image of an individual in two dimensions, in static form as opposed

Which is more creative?

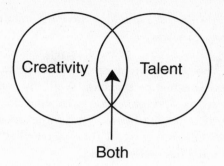

Creativity and talent are two different things. Sometimes they coexist.
This book is about developing your creativity. For ways to develop your
talent, go to the Yellow Pages and start with Arthur Murray Dance Studios.

to the living, breathing being that the portrait sitter was. This handsome individual's parents created him, and time and genetics dictated what he looked like at the time of this portrait. But the portrait itself shows no evidence of creativity on the painter's part. The portrait shows artistic talent documenting something that was already in existence, whereas the onion ring tree is a form I've never seen before. It is unique. It is a new idea manifested as a cheesy, plastic kitchen item. Hey, no one ever said creativity has to be pretty.

> *Creativity and talent are two distinct things that sometimes coexist.*

Many people don't take a shot at being creative because they're confused by these two notions. I hear it all the time: "I can't draw a straight line, I'm not creative." "I can't sing, I'm not creative." Singing is a talent. Drawing a straight line is a talent. Or you can use a ruler. But, maybe just thinking of a straight line is the solution to a problem no one's ever had before. Then that's creative. It takes no artistic talent

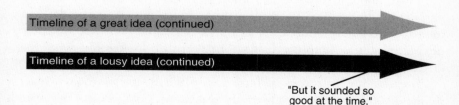

Timeline of a great idea (continued)

Timeline of a lousy idea (continued)

"But it sounded so good at the time."

to think of a straight line. Anyone can have the idea of a straight line, whether or not they can draw it.

This misconception is so pervasive in our society. I see it all the time. *Creative Needlework* is the name of a book of patterns from which you copy an idea that someone else had. Well, the person who initially had the idea was creative, but everyone else who has ever copied that pattern definitely was not performing anything creative in doing so. Even in a creative cooking class, if the master chef tells you exactly how to do it, you have to create nothing.

❦❦❦

THE CREATIVE DEPARTMENT?

I ran an ad agency creative department for many years at a company that went by many names, starting with Leonard/Monahan. All ad agencies have creative departments. I must say with a lack of humility usually reserved for parents that this creative department was one of the best in the world from the mid-1980s to mid-1990s, and I challenge anyone to argue that point. Schenck, Lubars, Baldwin and Goodrich, just to name the creative directors.

In addition to having some extremely creative people in the creative department, extremely talented people worked for me, too. All the people were a blend of both *creativity* and *talent*. But as creative as this department was, I would say that most of the people who worked for me were stronger on the talent side of the equation than the creative side. Nice writing. Well-crafted art. But where did the idea for the ad come from? My company probably exhibited the 80/20 rule as well as any ad agency in the business—that is, 80 percent of the big ideas come from 20 percent of the people. (See Chapter 18, Mind Farming, for a detailed discussion of creative personality typing.)

———————❖———————

I hear about creative artists, and I go to galleries, and so much of it has already been done. It's so derivative. Most fine art, particularly in the early periods—landscapes, still lifes, portraiture—is not a display of creativity. It is simply a display of talent. If it looked like what the artist was painting, they created nothing. They re-created it at best.

There's a fun little exercise I use quite often in my classroom to clarify the distinction between creativity and talent. I play a piece of music

This painting is not the result of creativity. It's the result of
artistic talent. If this scene looks like the vista that was
copied, then the painter created nothing. God created this
landscape. Or, ironically, if this were farmland, then a farmer
would have "created" much of it with a tractor. The artist with
the brush in this case exhibited talent, not creativity.
In fact, the artist here was my dad, and if I'm not mistaken
his "inspiration" was another painting.

written and first recorded by rocker Van Morrison when he was in a
British Invasion band called Them. The song is called "Gloria." As I
play that piece of music, I ask people to play rock 'n' roll trivia with me,
and in nearly every group, someone knows it's Van Morrison.

Then I immediately play a different version of the same song,
recorded by the American band, The Shadows of Night, who covered
the Van Morrison song and actually had a hit with it in 1967. Some
people guess this.

Then I play yet another version of the song, this time by rocker
Patti Smith who reinvents the song. If you've never heard it, not until
the chorus line of "Gloria" do you know it's that song — it's very different from the original.

Finally in this demonstration, I have a bunch of guys from my ad
agency singing "Gloria" on tape, and I play that for the group.

These four different "artists" demonstrate the four different combi-
nations of creativity and talent.

Van Morrison's clip demonstrates true creativity — after all, he
wrote the song. He has talent. He can hit the notes and remember the
words. I wish I could do that.

The Shadows of Night did not create the song. They did a cover.
But they hit the notes and remembered the words. They have musical
talent.

The artists*	Creativity	Talent
Van Morrison	✓	✓
The Shadows of Night	✗	✓
Patti Smith	✓	✗
Agency Guys Singing	✗	✗

The Creativity/Talent Scorecard
*Even the term *artist* is often confusing. Are all of these
talented people artists? Maybe. Are they all creative artists?
Well, no. Are they even all talents? Well, no again.

Patti Smith totally reinvented the song. She brought creativity to it. Is Patti a brilliant singer? I think not. But Patti Smith is in what I call the "Dylan strata." I know that some of you are about to throw this book at the wall, but I'll say it anyway: "Bob Dylan has very little musical talent."

ROCK 'N' ROLL BLASPHEMY

"But I like the way Dylan sings," some of you protest. Oh really? I will tell you that I believe that Dylan is one of the greatest minds in the history of rock 'n' roll—and maybe in contemporary art, period. He is extremely creative and has written some amazing songs. But I'm not convinced Dylan would have made it if he hadn't created his own songs. As much as you might say you like to hear Dylan sing, I'm not sure you'd pay the cover charge at the local Marriott lounge to hear a Bob Dylan who never wrote a song standing up there singing a Bee Gees medley of disco tunes.

We respect Dylan for his amazing creativity. We tolerate his lack of talent. He's an adequate guitar player. On a good day, he hits some notes with his voice. But, I'm sorry, he's a pretty horrible harmonica player; he makes even Neil Young sound good. Yes, we could argue that this is subjective. But, relative to Patti Smith, at the Rock and Roll Hall of Fame induction ceremonies in 2000, as she was inducting one of the greatest producers of all times, Clive Davis (founder of Arista Records), Patti herself confessed to her lack of talent, touting Davis as a visionary because she was the first artist he signed to Arista! "And I can't even sing," she said. She then went on to prove it through one of her more lively "primetime" performances.

Patti Smith is extremely creative, and on a good day she hits some notes. But if she didn't bring some creativity to the party, she, like Dylan, would have a hard time getting anyone to pay the $3.00 cover charge at the local Marriott lounge.

And finally, although the guys at my office might be creative and talented, it doesn't show up on their recording of "Gloria." All people exhibit creativeness and talent in different ways, and singing is not one of the talents that these fellows possess.

Are you beginning to see the lesson here? You don't need artistic talent to play in the creative game.

ABUSING TALENT

On the other side of the coin, this clarification should also raise a caution to people who use their immense artistic talents in tandem with mediocre or even lousy ideas. Just because it looks good, sounds good, or tastes good doesn't mean it's creative.

In advertising, I see so many wonderfully produced commercials and other advertisements that are well crafted and finely executed, but are they built around a great idea? Too often the answer is no. Advertising is an idea business. Craft doesn't change consumer perceptions the way a new idea does. It's the same in almost all industries: the nice-looking teapot that dribbles all over your linen tablecloth or the flaw-lessly executed financial service that offers customers absolutely no advantages over the competitor's product.

The confusion between creativity and talent works both ways. Once you understand the difference, you stand a better chance of not letting either misconception hold you back.

MICROSOFT IN THE HEAD ON THIS ONE

To point out the amazing degree to which the term *creativity* is misunderstood, when you look up the word *creative* in Microsoft Word's thesaurus, these are the synonyms you may choose from: *aesthetic, lovely, poetic, elegant, artistic, beautiful, decorative, musical,* and *patterned.*

Well, if Microsoft says creative means aesthetic, lovely, poetic, elegant, artistic, beautiful, decorative, musical, and patterned, that must be what the word means, right? You tell me. Did you pick up this book to become more aesthetic, lovely, poetic, elegant, artistic, beautiful, decorative, musical, and patterned? I didn't think so. Not that people don't buy books to become aesthetic, lovely, poetic, elegant, artistic, beautiful, decorative, musical, and patterned. I may have a few such books at home on my shelf. But did I expect these books on aesthetic, lovely, poetic, elegant, artistic, beautiful, decorative, musical, and patterned to make me more creative?

"They're only words," you may say. But most of us use words to define what we understand and believe, and if we're using all the wrong words we're making it really hard to change our limiting beliefs.

Cheat Notes for Chapter 4:
Creativity versus Talent

- *Creativity and talent are two distinct things that sometimes coexist.*

- *Artistic talent is mostly genetic. Everyone has the ability to think creatively.*

- *We all exhibit our creativeness and talent in different ways.*

- *You don't need artistic talent to be creative. You just need to have original ideas.*

- *Beware the impressions given by the expression of talent; just because it looks good, sounds good, or tastes good doesn't mean it's creative.*

PART III

Tools for the Job of Thinking Creatively

Here in Part III I offer a number of creative thinking tools to help you with your Do-It-Yourself Lobotomy. I have been developing and working with these tools over the years with thousands upon thousands of people. Each of these tools is a codified mental process. They are all based on methods and patterns of thinking exhibited by some of the world's greatest thinkers since the beginning of time.

To better understand how these thinking tools work, let's look at the more tangible physical realm. There are some very basic physical tools that have helped people with achievement on that plane since time immemorial, body mechanics such as hip flexing, arm extending, and shoulder rotating, to name a few. Many of the top achievers in the physical realm, athletes, for instance, work with general physical trainers to hone these physical tools. For instance, baseball great Nomar Garciaparra (who, incidentally, used his version of my 180° Thinking tool to change his name from Ramon to Nomar, by spelling it backward), uses the same physical trainer as pro athletes in other sports. The trainer works on the basics of physical mechanics to maximize athletic performance. The trainer doesn't show Nomar how to throw a baseball better, but rather works on his mechanics and helps fine-tune his tools so that he *can* throw a baseball better.

Similarly, some basic mind mechanics can be used in various thinking situations with great results. Whether you're an advertising copywriter or a real estate tycoon, a product marketing manager or a chemist, the mechanics of my Do-It-Yourself Lobotomy tools cross all disciplines to improve your effectiveness.

These techniques are particularly powerful if you use them consciously and consistently, which is what this book will help you do.

If Nomar used the mechanics he learned from his physical trainer only once or twice, would he expect big results? Certainly not. And would Nomar use these mechanics if they were difficult to use, complex, and time-consuming? Well, he probably would, because he's an extraordinarily driven athlete. But for the average person, the breaking down of the physical mechanics into simple, easy-to-use, foolproof tools is the most effective pathway to success. That is why I have synthesized basic aspects of the creative thinking processes into very uncomplicated elements, given them simple mechanics (and I use the term loosely), easy-to-remember descriptive names, and made them very easy to use in almost any situation.

UNIVERSAL TOOLS

In the same way that similar body movements can be used for different activities (e.g., the hip motion used in hitting a baseball, swinging a golf club, or throwing a javelin), similar mind mechanics can be used in creating web sites, exploring medical cures, and improving retail customer service. That, of course, is why these tools are so universal — and why they can be effective for you, no matter what field you are in.

For years I have been working with people, mostly (but not exclusively) in business. These tools have been used effectively in food service, technology, packaged goods, finance, entertainment . . . it might be easier to name the fields in which these tools *haven't* been applied. Since the beginning, I have been getting feedback from individuals and groups on how effective these tools have been for finding fresh ideas and solving problems. I have personally witnessed or heard firsthand accounts of literally thousands of cases where these tools helped people think bigger and find better ideas. You can rest assured that this is not just theory. This is the sharing of proven, effective methods of thinking that you can bring to bear in your job and your life every day.

THE SURGICAL INSTRUMENTS OF THE
DO-IT-YOURSELF LOBOTOMY

Every one of the tools we're about to discuss will help you perform a Do-It-Yourself Lobotomy, each in a somewhat different way. The common thread is that they are all designed to help you let go of what you know. As we discussed conceptually in the opening chapters, attachment to the known holds most people back from finding better ideas. When you use the simple tools explained in this book, with little effort you will be able to circumvent, or lobotomize, the area of your mind that knows the answer.

Only when you ask a better question will you get a better answer. When you speed through many ideas using 100 MPH Thinking, you *will* have more fresh ideas. When you use Intergalactic Thinking, by definition, you will bring your thoughts to a different place. When you take the 180° Thinking route, well . . . nah, I don't want to spoil it all for you. I want you to experience 180° Thinking for yourself in that chapter ahead.

TOOLS WITH STRONG HANDLES

Part of the reason these tools are so effective is the kind of names I've given them. Descriptive, memorable, and fairly short names such as 100 MPH Thinking, Intergalactic Thinking, Ask a Better Question, and 180° Thinking simply make the tools they represent easier to use.

I was using each of these thinking methods long before I started naming them. And you know what? They weren't quite as effective, neither for individuals nor, particularly, for groups. People understood the concepts, but they often had a hard time communicating what the tools meant to others, which also affected how they used the thinking methods themselves.

The names help you quickly get your mind around the basic functions of the tools. For groupthink, these mnemonic handles facilitate quicker, easier communication, to be sure. Imagine hearing a team of carpenters talking about their tools if they didn't have names for them: "Hey, Bob, can you pass me that long, flat, tapered piece of sheet metal with the sharp teeth and the wooden handle?" I don't think so.

A number of years ago the head of AT&T new media told me he had a bunch of creative geniuses working for him. When I asked if they could speak to each other in the same language he looked at me sideways, as if to say, "There's a language?"

Yes, there is a language. It's the names of these tools. When teams use these methods for groupthink, it's like a football team calling a play. Someone says, "Let's throw some 180° Thinking at this opportunity," and everyone else knows the drill. Imagine even the best football players in the world going out on a field with no set plays. They'd all be running into each other.

The names make the tools more usable. They give them handles. We're a sound-bite society that needs shortcuts to communicate. When it comes to creative thinking, you now have your vocabulary.

Open Your Mind

Of course, nothing in life comes without some conditions, right? Here's the catch to learning these tools that make opening your mind easier and more fruitful than ever before: You may need to open your mind just to learn them.

> *As with learning almost anything as an adult, it means you must let go of some of your existing beliefs and practices—that is, those beliefs and practices that may run counter to the new material you're learning.*

Then again, since we demonstrated earlier that in many ways you've been an unconscious thinker for most of your life, maybe it shouldn't be so hard to learn these different ways of thinking after all.

Changing old thinking habits and thought patterns is an entirely different thing. It will require some discipline to use the new tools regularly, to keep you out of your old ruts and to make you more at home in new, more bountiful grooves of thinking. To that end, we'll provide some guidance at the end of Part III to help you integrate these new methods into your life for maximum long-term results.

As I mentioned earlier in this book, many of the thought methods that are used here are things you already do on your best days. You just do them less consciously now than you will after you learn about them in the next few chapters. As I also mentioned earlier, this section is less of a learning exercise than it is a "recognizing" experience.

So sit back and open your mind. The Do-It-Yourself Lobotomy tools are the meat of this book. Eat it up. Digest it. And let it help you satisfy your hunger for creative thinking for the rest of your life.

Ask a Better Question

The first creative thinking power tool I'd like to cover is a concept that I call Ask a Better Question. Let me introduce you to it through an exercise I do with the groups that I lead in my workshops.

Look at this picture. This is a picture of me. I want you to answer this question in the blank spaces below. What am I wearing? (Come on, play along. You'll learn something, I promise.)

What am I wearing?

———————————————————————

———————————————————————

———————————————————————

You probably wrote something like "dark suit, neutral shirt, dark tie," maybe "black shoes." You knew all the answers. You were "in the known." There was little place for your imagination. What you *don't* know, however, is what kind of socks I am wearing. In the blanks below, I want you to venture some guesses about what kind of socks I might be wearing.

———————————————————————

———————————————————————

———————————————————————

_____

_____

    Now I want to ask a more specific question. What might the design be on my socks? If you haven't already done so, write down some designs that come to mind. If you already wrote down some designs, write down a few more in the following blanks.

_____

_____

_____

_____

_____

    Next question: What's an unusual design that you wouldn't expect to find on socks?

_____

_____

_____

_____

_____

    Last question: What's a highly unusual design that you would never, ever expect to find on socks? Push it out. Come on, write down that crazy thought that crossed your mind. It's all right, I won't tell anyone.

_____

_____

_____

_____

_____

What do you see?

Something you've seen hundreds of times before.
Something so common and ordinary that there's
almost nothing to look at. Well, turn this page upside
down and see what you see. Then go to the next
spread to see how a fresh perspective can
sometimes make all the difference in the world.

BETTER QUESTIONS: PUSHING BEYOND THE KNOWN

Let's talk about the answers to my questions, both your answers and the answers I get in my workshops. Of course, for the first question about what I am wearing, you knew the answer. Black suit. Neutral shirt. And so on. The known. However, when you had to wonder, when you had to engage your imagination, that was a different story.

To the second question, "What kind of socks might I be wearing?" in my workshops the first answer I usually hear is "black socks." Big surprise. Black suit, black shoes, black socks. Wow! I also often hear wool or Gold Toe. Sometimes I hear designs—argyle, paisley, polka dots, stripes.

If I haven't heard designs and people are kind of stifled, then I ask the third question, "What's the design on my socks?" If they weren't mentioned already, I tend to hear the usual suspects. Argyle. Paisley. Stripes. Polka dots.

When I ask, "What's an unusual design you wouldn't expect to find on socks?" I often hear topical things. Around Christmastime, I hear "Christmas trees," "Santa Claus." Around World Series time I hear "baseballs," "Babe Ruth." During the O.J. Simpson trial, I heard "Nicole's blood" (yuck!). I often hear topical things and sometimes I hear things like "fish," "flowers," "race cars." These are unusual designs.

Finally, I ask the question, "What's a highly unusual design you would *never, ever* expect to find on socks?" Typically, that's when people start using their imaginations and coming up with things that they haven't seen or are unlikely to see. They push it out: flying elephants . . . neckties on socks . . . Bela Lugosi in a swimsuit.

Yes, the imagination often comes up with some pretty amazing possibilities when pushed. Again, the exercise illustrates a thinking tool. A creative thinking tool. A Do-It-Yourself Lobotomy tool called Ask a Better Question.

IT STARTS WITH THE QUESTION

Suppose I started with this question, "What's a highly unusual design that you would never expect to find on socks?"

Would I have heard "black" or "Gold Toe" or "knee-high"? No. Would I have heard "argyle, paisley, stripes" if I had asked for an unusual design? Not on your life. You see, in my workshops, and prob-

Music: Hendrix in
a 21st-century
kind of way.

Camera tilts up to
top of bottle.

Hand twists cap off
and places on bottle
upside down.

Music pauses as
you slap yourself
upside the head.

A gazillion people have looked at the Bud bottle cap (20 gazillion if you count college kids). Then someone takes a fresh look and the King of Beers is officially crowned. The lesson: Never stop looking for the fresh perspective. This is one of the freshest Bud spots in years. Go figure.

ably on these worksheets, the early answers tend to be pretty lame. And I'll take the blame, because I was asking pretty lame questions. I was asking questions that allowed you to stay in the known. It's human nature to want to know the answer. Since our childhood years we've always strived to know *the* answer, and *the* answer is something that already exists, so we tend to go with what already exists. Besides, saying "Bela Lugosi in a swimsuit" without permission is really putting yourself out there. If you immediately answered, "Bela-Lugosi-in-a-swimsuit socks!" I might even think you're a little strange, and I'm the creative thinking coach who's trying to get you to think out of the box.

The mind is capable of imagining much more than what you know, particularly if encouraged to do so. It's just that we tend to put ourselves in a predefined context in terms of solving problems or answering questions. This determines how we approach a situation. We put ourselves in a context that can be addressed with a known, but when asked progressively more probing questions, you had no choice but to push your mind out to a place you've never been before. By definition, the question forced you there.

This Lobotomy tool, as I stated, is called Ask a Better Question. It's been around since the beginning of time. Wasn't that the Socratic method? Questions?

Questions have caused people to think better for years. When you asked a question in college, didn't your best professors answer with a question? Why? Because that made you think.

> *Some of the greatest thinkers of all time have asked great questions. You, when you're at your creative best, ask great questions, too.*

Better Question/Better Ad

I received this lesson early in my advertising career. I was working on the first tennis shoe commercial to air on television. It was a product owned by Colgate-Palmolive, called the Fred Perry tennis shoe. And I remember when research told us . . . drumroll . . . "comfort" was the major benefit of this shoe. "Okay," the other creative team members and I said with a deflated sigh. "Okay. Comfort. Big deal." But then the entire team, account people and creatives, started asking better ques-

The Lobotomy Files

Bite Me Live Bait®, Thinking 180° to Port.

Arkwear is one of the top tourist apparel outlets in the busy seaside city of Newport, Rhode Island. On a sunny summer afternoon we are constantly restocking our most popular designs to keep pace with our customers.

In 1997, in an effort to make our T-shirts, hats and other souvenir apparel stand out from the cluttered local tourist offerings, we decided to use 180° Thinking. Figuring that virtually all of the other local souvenir garment designers were featuring beautiful sailboats in the surf and other classic, nautical Newport icons on their clothing, why not go in the opposite direction and show the barnacle-crusted fishing heritage of the real Newport? The Bite Me Live Bait brand was born and became an immediate success with our customers. It has since achieved a sort of pop-culture notoriety as its own brand, in many ways eclipsing our highly successful, more established Arkwear brand. The Bite Me Live Bait brand has continued to grow and prosper in recent years to the point where it now has its own website, bitemelivebait.com, featuring Bite Me Live Bait sweatshirts, baseball caps and coffee mugs, beyond the original tourist apparel scope, bringing in business from around the world.

Jeff Marlowe
President, Arkwear
Lobotomized 1995

For more on 180° Thinking, go to Chapter 8.

tions. Why do you need to be comfortable? Because you run all over the tennis court. Forward. Backward. Side to side. Lateral. Linear. Jumping. Turning.

How much of that do you do? Good question. "How far do you think you run?" asked Bruce Leonard, a great marketing mind with whom I later went into business. *That* was a better question.

That question put us in a place where we didn't know the answer, where we had no choice but to wonder. And then we found the answer. Are you ready for this? In a long match, a single tennis player can run as much as five miles. Now that's a surprising premise. That puts comfort in a very important position. The creative execution we chose—to paint the soles of a guy's tennis shoes and have him run around the tennis court leaving five miles of footprints—was a very interesting TV spot. And it worked! Colgate ran the ad for nine years. Veterans of the ad biz may remember *AdAge's* top 100 TV spots. This commercial made that coveted list in the 1970s.

Someone asked a better question. It led to a better answer. We all do this on our best days. Do we do it consciously? Do we do it intentionally? Do we do it consistently? Now that you are more aware that this is a fundamental of creative thinking, maybe you can use this technique to lobotomize the part of your brain that comes up with the same old answers. By pushing yourself beyond the known, you might just get a better idea.

❧❁❦

BETTER QUESTIONS ON TOP OF BETTER QUESTIONS

Once I was leading a brainstorming group for a major computer manufacturer, and we were exploring better phone support for their consumer PC line. As you may understand, computers sold to people in business are acquired by a central purchaser (IT, MIS, whatever) who is computer-savvy and purchases thousands of units. In offering phone support for such people, you can speak their language. But in offering phone support for home users, you have to take a different approach. We were well into the brainstorming session and coming up with hundreds of ideas, some of them quite good, when someone asked, "How about if we assume the person at the other end of the line is five years old? Wouldn't that cause us to make different assumptions and approach this phone support differently?" Well, let me tell you, a lot of people's eyes lit up. Yes! Because the people calling for support on home computers are not sophisticated, let's assume they're five years old. (This was around 1995 when the PC market was in steep growth.) But a few minutes later someone else said, "Wait a minute. Aren't kids coming out of the womb pointing and clicking? Maybe we don't assume the people on the other end of the line are five years old. Maybe we assume they're 75 years old. Because aren't those the techno-phobes?" (I'm not sure they still are, but back then this group had not yet embraced the computer. Today, I believe, it's one of the growing categories of home PC sales.)

Asking a better question, then asking an even better question, led to some much better answers.

❖

You can ask a better question at any point in time, at any point in the creative process. Of course, I prefer *starting* at a better place.

In fact, if you think about it, it's an instant lobotomy: If you are using the part of the brain that thinks about socks as paisley, argyle, and all the usual suspects and thinks about tennis shoes as arch support, padding, traction, and all the usual comfort things, then asking a better question will put you in a place *where you don't have the answer.* What's a highly unusual design? I don't know. How far does somebody run? I don't know. When you put yourself in that place, you lobotomize yourself and put yourself in a place of wonder—that place where wonderful things happen.

THE BENEFITS OF ASKING A BETTER QUESTION

One benefit is that when you ask the right kind of question it triggers curiosity. I study high-achieving creative people, and the highest-achieving creative people of all time are tremendously curious. Leonardo da Vinci showed great curiosity: How do birds fly? How do fish swim underwater? Thomas Edison was tremendously curious. Curiosity means putting yourself in a place you don't know. Putting yourself in a place of wonder. (Don't we often praise bright people with the compliment, "She knows what she doesn't know"?)

Timeline of a great idea (continued)

Timeline of a lousy idea (continued)

Maybe you shouldn't have been so quick to commit to that no-one-will-notice-if-I-slip-it-through idea.

You were at your best creatively when you were young and didn't know anything. As a child, you were extremely curious. You lived in your imagination nearly 100 percent of the time. But today, as an adult, you know so much. Well, the Ask a Better Question technique can put you in a position to know less and to be more curious and therefore more creative.

CREATIVE PROBLEM CAUSING IN ACTION

We talk about problems causing us to stretch, and we mention that we're at our best when we are stretching. Like the athlete whose highlights film shows him stretching, your resume shows you stretching. However, the athlete has to wait for the ball to be just out of reach, or seemingly out of reach, in order to be able to stretch and make the "impossible" play, whereas you can "place the solution just out of your reach" by simply asking the right question. You can cause yourself to stretch any time you want.

Think about it. When you have a dilemma, when you have a problem to solve, what do you tend to do? You tend to look for an answer that you know. I can guarantee you'll get more creative results if you ask a better question. All you have to do is pose a question for which you don't know the answer.

A number of years ago I was working with a major dairy, looking for more effective ways to sell milk, a commodity item to be sure. I challenged the group with this question: "Assume because of some manufacturing problem or other problem your price is twice that of your competitor. Now how do you get people to buy your milk?" They were pushing their minds in 100 different directions because they didn't know the answer to that question. They hadn't experienced that kind of a problem. They had no choice but to stretch. And it all started with someone asking a better question.

❧❀❧

HOW TO ASK A BETTER QUESTION

When I first started my creative coaching, I was working with a TV station whose news numbers were very low compared to the competition. I remember taking a group of executives into a brainstorming session and separating them into four or five smaller teams of five people or so (see Chapter 19 for tips on group brainstorming). I began by posing questions about how to improve the news—questions that made them stretch their minds:

How do we do a newscast in one minute?
How do we do a newscast with no anchors?
How do we do a newscast with no sound?
How do we do a newscast for 24 hours with no repeats?

This Ask a Better Question process forced them into places where they didn't "know" the answers. If you look at the questions, you'll see that a lot of the answers I was trying to elicit were graphical in nature. In a short amount of time you have to get a lot of data on the screen. If there's no audio, you have to get data on the screen. If you have no anchors, there has to be something on the screen.

Little did I know how prophetic was my exercise. If you look at newscasts today compared to 10 to 15 years ago, the whole industry has gone in that direction. People are quicker on the uptake today and take in greater amounts of data with more ease than ever before. The whole world is more graphic today, more jam-packed with information. Just look at a 30-year-old episode of *The Mary Tyler Moore Show* or *The Andy Griffith Show*. Things move faster, there's more editing, more information jammed in. I bet if you did a word count on dialogue in today's sitcoms versus those of 30 years ago, you'd find about 30 percent more words. But I digress.

These TV station executives glimpsed the future when they stretched their minds. By not looking at how things "are," they clarified their forward vision.

Well, there is some good news, some bad news, and some sad news in the outcome to this story. The good news is that the TV station made some changes and soon overtook their nearest competitor in the ratings war. The bad news is that they got cold feet on immediate implementation of many of the leading-edge ideas that emerged from this brainstorming session. The sad news is that the general manager of this TV station, the visionary who was leading the charge, died suddenly. The station has been mired in poor ratings ever since, currently under their fourth general manager in six years.

Many of the ideas we came up with in that session are commonplace today. The news ticker on the bottom of the screen. Time and temperature in the lower corner. The station logo as a permanent bug in the other corner, and so on. This group saw the future when they stretched their thinking, thanks to Ask a Better Question. You can, too!

❖

Cheat Notes for Chapter 5:
Ask a Better Question

- The mind is capable of imagining much more than "what you know," particularly if encouraged to do so by a probing question.

- Probing questions offer no choice but to push your mind to a place you've never been before, a place of wonder where wonderful things can happen.

- Cause yourself to stretch anytime by placing the solution just out of reach, by posing a question in such a manner that you don't know the answer.

- You can ask a better question at any point in time during the creative process.

Ask the Question Early

There's a variation on Ask a Better Question that in some ways is actually a better tool than Ask a Better Question itself. It's what I call Ask the Question Early.

Before I explain this tool, let's talk about human nature. Let me ask you, if you have something due next Thursday, when do you start it? Be honest. You're thinking, "I'll start it Wednesday," right? Or, you may be thinking, "When is it due Thursday? Late in the day? Maybe I can start early Thursday."

Well you're not alone.

It's often human nature to wait until the last minute to do something. I propose that, even if you're not going to start working on the project until the day before it's due, you visit the problem now. Consciously. Spend 20 minutes with it now. Ask the question early. It will get your imagination perking.

> *The best thinkers ask the question early, giving themselves many opportunities to be inspired.*

How long does it take to find the solution to a problem? Quite often, it's a nanosecond, but let's use a full second as our unit of measure. If you start a day ahead of time, you have 86,400 seconds. If you formulate your question a week ahead of time, you have 604,800 seconds to work with, over half a million extra opportunities to come up with a big idea. If you need to score a touchdown, do you want 30 seconds on the clock or three minutes? To ask is to answer.

TICK. TICK. TICK. TICK. TICK. TICK.

The great irony is that when you ask the question early you don't have to work on it. Your subconscious mind will work on the problem. Your subconscious mind is working at levels you have no awareness of. That and your superconscious mind are tapping into all that's around you. At a conscious rate we can process only 120 to 130 bits of data every second, but on a subconscious or superconscious level we can process millions of bits of data. For example, perhaps a bird flies by and triggers a thought that can be the solution to a problem. If you haven't asked the question, you don't know that the bird is the inspiration for the solution to your problem. You can become inspired only if you know what the problem is.

You already do this on your best days. Don't you get ideas out of nowhere? Seemingly out of nowhere, that is. When you're driving in the car or exercising or waking in the morning, you get ideas "out of the blue" quite often. But, wait a minute, you can't find a solution to a problem you're unaware of. You asked the question early, whether you did it consciously or not. And if you didn't do it consciously and you're just relying on happenstance, well, you're lucky you asked the question early. If you do it consciously, if you take this thinking tool seriously and integrate this practice into your work style and spend 20 minutes with the problem a week ahead of time (if you have the luxury), or just spend five minutes a day ahead for that matter, you heighten your odds of having better ideas.

This is a time management thing. You have all the time in the world to do your job, right?

Wrong.

Anybody who's been in business for a number of years knows that you have less time today than you had two years ago. (Do you remember the old days of the twentieth century? Remember how slow the pace was then?) Two years from now you'll have even less time than today. The world is spinning faster and faster. We have less and less time. This creative thinking tool — Ask the Question Early — is a way to manage your time, to get more out of your thinking. When you ask the question early, consciously, you give yourself many more opportunities to be inspired, many more opportunities to have that flash of brilliance that so often happens when you're looking to solve a problem (or often when you're *not* looking). And, as with so many of the Do-It-Yourself Lobotomy tools we'll cover in this book, it's easy to do, it doesn't cost a penny, and it will make you a better thinker.

Cheat Notes for Chapter 6:
Ask the Question Early

- *When you ask the question early you don't have to work on the problem now; your subconscious mind will work on it for you.*

- *So even if you're not going to start working on the project until the day before it's due, visit the problem now.*

- *Asking the question early will get your imagination perking, giving you many more opportunities to be inspired.*

- *If you Ask a Better Question and spend 20 minutes with the problem a week (or a day) ahead of time, you greatly increase your odds of having better ideas.*

100 MPH Thinking: Thinking at the Speed of Enlightenment

If you're looking for an easy, foolproof way to come up with big ideas, try a technique that's so basic to creative thinking that it's been practiced by some of the world's greatest thinkers since time began. It's a process I call 100 MPH Thinking.

First let me explain how you do it: You come up with lots of ideas in a short amount of time.

Let me repeat that. Because it sounds much too simple. *You come up with lots of ideas in a short amount of time.* Actually, you come up with lots and lots of ideas in a short, short amount of time.

Gee, it still sounds pretty simple. Could that be because it *is* simple? Could be.

Well, let's try to make it a bit more complicated, so it will feel like a much greater accomplishment when you master it.

> *100 MPH Thinking is an ideation method that combines two fundamental concepts of creative thinking:* quantity *and* speed.

Quantity simply means that you make as your goal the *number* of ideas and not the quality of ideas. I believe that it's much easier to come up with 50 ideas than it is to come up with *the* perfect idea. And I believe it's nearly impossible to come up with 50 bad ideas. The sheer quantity almost ensures that some *have* to be good. I mean, even a blind squirrel can find a nut if he looks in enough places.

And I believe it's easier to come up with 50 good ideas *quickly* (say in 15 minutes) than it is to do it over a longer amount of time. But I seem to have sped ahead of myself here. Let's look at that quantity thing a bit more closely.

You'll Have Better Ideas . . . It's the Law

The quantity concept is based on a simple mathematical principle—the law of large numbers. While a mathematician might state this law more complexly, I look at it with a sort of Forrest Gump profundity: "If you come up with more ideas, you'll *have* more ideas."

If the law of large numbers were applied to baseball, we'd all be great hitters, because we'd have unlimited swings at the ball, not a mere three strikes. If applied to the stock market or Las Vegas, the law of large numbers would make us all winners, because we could put our money on as many potential opportunities as we'd like. But baseball and Wall Street and the roulette table at Caesar's Palace give us finite limitations. Conversely, when it comes to generating ideas, we can take as many shots as we want. There are absolutely no limitations, except maybe time. That's where thinking fast comes in.

Speed Doesn't Kill

Coming up with lots of ideas very quickly offers many benefits.

Speed gives you momentum of thought, which silences the judge, circumvents fear, and makes failure less painful. "Get that root canal over with quickly, please."

But mostly, speed gets you to the large number of ideas quicker.

Let's slow down and look at those many benefits of thinking quickly.

The Silence of the Judge
Judging is one of the worst things you can do when ideating.

> *I believe when you take the time to judge each idea as it exits the birth canal of your mind, you lose, whether you think the idea is good or bad.*

Here's what happens. You come up with an idea and judge it. If it's a bad idea, how does that make you feel? "Oh, no. I'm a bum. I'll never

Small and nimble
versus

Big and lumbering

This commercial for EDS,
"The running of the squirrels,"
created by Fallon McElligott,
Minneapolis, parodies the
annual "Running of the Bulls"
in Pamplona, Spain. The spot
is a classic use of 180°
Thinking, showing the dangers
of the small, nimble competitor
as being perhaps more
threatening to business today
than the large, more lumbering
competition. (For more on
180° Thinking see Chapter 8.)

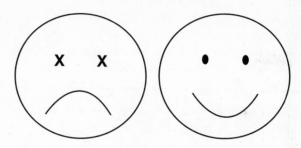

With negative judgment you lose. With
positive judgment you lose.

come up with a great idea." That's a good state of mind for developing brilliant ideas? I don't think so.

Or let's say you judge your idea to be good. Then what? What do you think most people do when they find a good idea? That's right. They stop looking. They're happy, so they stop. "I have a good idea. I have a solution to my problem. Thank you. I'll get on to the next crisis that needs my genius."

Sorry, friends, but that attitude is the attitude of the great gray masses. Not the attitude of the big winners. In an age when it takes major advancements to get an edge and huge ideas to create impact, what good are merely good ideas? As Voltaire said, "Good is the enemy of great."

Again, the reason most people don't come up with great ideas is because they come up with good ideas, then they stop. Is there a better idea? You'll never know if you stop.

So you see, judgment during the early phases of creative thinking screws things up either way. My suggestion? Use 100 MPH Thinking to come up with many ideas—10 ideas, 50 ideas, 100 ideas. Why not? Heck, if you normally come up with two or three ways to solve a problem, 10 is 300 to 500 percent greater. And 50 is something like 1,800 to 2,500 percent better. And 100 ideas? Well that's whole magnitudes better than two or three ideas!

When you come up with your 10, 50, or 100 ideas, then you judge them. Who cares how many are less than perfect, or downright horrible for that matter. Are two pretty good? Maybe five? Perhaps eight? What's wrong with that?

> I get twenty ideas for songs to get one finished. I get twenty songs finished to get one worth singing to someone else. I get twenty worth singing by me to get one which somebody else finds worth singing.
>
> Pete Seeger

If you're going to tell me, "Yeah, but that means the majority are lousy," then I'm sorry, pal, but you're seeing the idea font half empty. Who cares how many are bad! Some are pretty damn good, maybe even great. That's all you should care about.

> *The best baseball players, guys with batting averages of .300, still fail 7 out of 10 times.*

The best scientists fail more than the average scientists. The best films have miles of outtakes on the editing room floor. Get over this desire for perfection. It can't be achieved.

⚜

FERTILIZER

I often hear people who think they understand creativity say things like, "There's no such thing as a bad idea."

Are they kidding?

There are bad ideas all around us. There are horrible ideas that stay ideas, never making it out of the concept realm to be executed, thank heaven. Lousy ideas also come to fruition that at best never have a chance at succeeding and at worst put companies out of business.

I have no problem with bad ideas in the conceptual stage. In fact, I think they're a healthy part of the creative process.

Let me tell you why.

I often hear people refer to bad ideas as *crap*, and that's the polite word. Actually, I think that description is pretty close, but I like to use a more constructive term: *fertilizer.*

Fertilizer helps things grow.

When people generate tons of ideas using 100 MPH Thinking, believe me, they are not all great ideas. In fact, most of the time a very small percentage are decent ideas, and an even smaller proportion are actually good ideas. But the other ideas act as fertilizer.

When I'm facilitating a group brainstorming session (see page 206), I can often look across a large room at many teams ideating, and from a distance I can tell you which groups have the best ideas. It's the groups with the most ideas. Oh, sure, they also have the most bad ideas, but that means they have more fertilizer.

Often, when running a workshop or brainstorming session, I offer a prize to the team that generates the most ideas. Offering a prize as an incentive often gets the competitive juices flowing. "The prize," I tell the groups, "is an Automatic Idea Generator." Sometimes I get side-ways looks.

When all is said and done and we tally the quantitative output of each team, the team with the greatest number of ideas wins the prize. My Automatic Idea Generator? I pull it out of my pocket. It's a garbage bag. The message? If you can fill this, you'll have lots of ideas.

You see, there's a positive correlation between fertilizer and a bountiful harvest of ideas. The best films always have miles of footage on the cutting room floor. The best CDs have music you've never heard. The best books have chapters you've never read and characters you've never met. The best ad makers have dozens, if not hundreds, of tissues littering their floors. Many of these outtakes wind up in the garbage. All served as fertilizer.

I pulled this little prank when working with ad agency GSD&M in Austin, Texas, a few years ago. When I went back to their offices later in the day, large, galvanized trash barrels dotted the floor space. Seems the agency's president, Roy Spence, liked the garbage metaphor so well he wanted to encourage his people to throw away bad, even just decent, ideas in the pursuit of great ideas.

❖

HOW TO GET OVER YOUR F-f-f-EAR OF F-f-f-AILURE

There is probably nothing that holds people back from coming up with ideas more than, well (and I look over both shoulders as I say this), you know . . . *fear.*

Well, would it comfort you to know that fear is actually a good sign when pursuing things creative? It really comes down to fear of the unknown, because we're not sure this idea is good, that it will work, that others will like it. Well, if we were sure of those things, that would mean the idea has been done before, which may alleviate our fear, but it's also confirmation that the idea is not particularly creative.

Fear is part of the creative process. As is the great unknown. It's the place where true exploration and subsequent advancement take place.

"Yes, son, I was the one who thought of the big idea that led to that new division."

Timeline of a great idea (continued) ⟶

Timeline of a lousy idea (continued) ⟶

FAILURE NEVER FAILS

Of all the things we are afraid of, when it comes to new ideas, failure is the top dog. And it's a rabid Doberman. But 100 MPH Thinking is a way to tame this wild beast called failure. Because 100 MPH Thinking builds failure into the process.

When you come up with 10, 20, or 50 ideas, you're allowed to fail 9, 19, or 49 times, yet still succeed. The highest-achieving people know this, or at least they practice this.

Babe Ruth struck out more than anyone else in his era. Michael Jordan missed more shots than the players he opposed. Thomas Edison failed thousands of times on the way to finding the best filament for the lightbulb.

Not only does 100 MPH Thinking allow for failure, but it builds failure into the process (see Chapter 20, "The Five Greatest Barriers to Creativity").

> Show me someone who has never failed, and I'll show you someone who hasn't tried hard enough.
>
> Albert Einstein

I worked with a bunch of aerospace engineers a while back who seemed to grasp one of the benefits of 100 MPH Thinking quite esoterically, with the concept they call "fail-fast."

SIMPLY BRILLIANT

It's true that 100 MPH Thinking is not rocket surgery, as they like to say at the Bizarro chapter of Mensa. One of the biggest mistakes people make with this creative thinking tool is to overthink it and make it more complex than it is.

Come up with more ideas and you'll have more ideas. Do it quickly and you'll reap many other benefits. The secret is to not think about it. As those great philosophers at Nike tell us, "Just do it."

That great failure, Thomas Edison, who registered 1,093 patents in his amazingly productive career as an inventor, said, "It's not inspiration, it's perspiration." I'll add my own twist to that statement and say, "With 100 MPH Thinking, coming up with great ideas is no sweat."

> You miss 100% of the shots you don't take.
>
> Hockey great Wayne Gretsky

How to Use 100 MPH Thinking

Here's how to use 100 MPH Thinking in a group session (or 300 MPH Thinking if you're really looking for a thrill):

Step 1. Break down the number of people you have into teams of three to five players, max.

Step 2. Set a time limit and an ambitious number of ideas. Anywhere from 30 ideas per team in 10 minutes to 100 ideas per team in an hour.

Step 3. Write down all ideas (those little yellow stickies are perfect) and say each idea out loud to your team.

Step 100. When you reach your goal, have every team member select her or his top two or three ideas, compare notes with other teams, then debate or arm-wrestle until you have *the* idea you're looking for. (For a slightly more civilized method of distilling and finding agreement, see page 213 in Chapter 19, "Storming the Brain.")

❖

Cheat Notes for Chapter 7:
100 MPH Thinking

- *100 MPH Thinking combines two fundamental principles of creative thinking: quantity and speed.*

- *When exploring new ideas, aim for quantity; the quality will emerge. Aiming for quality alone is very difficult.*

- *When you come up with 10, 20, or 50 ideas, you're allowed to fail 9, 19, or 49 times, yet still succeed.*

- *Speed gives you momentum of thought, silences the judge, and circumvents fear.*

- *But mostly, speed gets you to the large number of ideas quicker.*

- *Get over the desire for perfection; it can't be achieved.*

- *The secret of 100 MPH Thinking is to not think too hard; just generate ideas.*

180° Thinking: A Tnereffid Way to Ideate

Whether or not we are aware of it, when we start out looking for new, bigger, better ideas in any field we are most often influenced by arbitrary boundaries of thought that severely limit our creative playing field.

When people in the bedding industry, for example, think of improving beds, they make many assumptions about its necessary properties: shape, materials, height, degree of levelness, temperature, measure of softness or firmness, color, texture, sounds it makes or doesn't make, and so on.

Most of these assumptions come directly from what has been done before in this category. Are these suppositions right? Are they the best answers? Are there better routes to take our thinking? We'll never know if we are slaves to those presumptions, even if we are conscious of the limits they put on us.

A thinking tool I have been working with and refining for years helps people escape the gravity of these limiting assumptions that hold back so many thinkers. It's a tool that not only chooses to ignore all of the preconceptions in any category of thinking, it actually uses those knowns as pushing-off points to change the direction of thinking by 180°, in much the same way lap swimmers use the end of the pool to propel themselves in the opposite direction. Not surprisingly, I call this method of ideation 180° Thinking.

AGAINST YOUR BETTER JUDGMENT

When faced with a problem to solve or anytime you'd like to apply some creative juice, simply direct your thought process in the exact

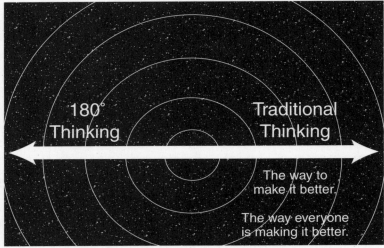

180° Thinking is simply the opposite of traditional thinking,
the way that everyone else is thinking to "make it better."

opposite direction of where conventional wisdom would suggest you go. *That* is 180° Thinking.

Going back to our bed example, if conventional wisdom says "soft," think "hard." If conventional wisdom says "warm," think "cold." If conventional wisdom says "low," think "high." Whatever you do, don't think of more ways to do soft, warm, and low. Not that there is anything wrong with those properties. And no one is to say there aren't better ways of doing those tried-and-true things with beds. It's just that those paths of thought are likely being followed by most other thinkers in this category. Because so many others are applying their creative energy there, those areas are likely to be a bit overfarmed for ideas.

You want to find different ideas? Look in a different place.

Creativity Is a Matter of Degree

Of course, you could make your thinking 90° different, or 10° or 17½° different. And, yes, those might be fresh pathways of thought. But I like 180° Thinking because it's usually easier to determine the exact opposite of something than to find 10° of difference. The opposite of a soft bed is a hard bed. Easy. What's 10° from soft? I'm not really sure.

The Lobotomy Files

Show, Don't Tell

We were looking for a good promotional handle to introduce a new customer service idea for a major client, a supermarket chain down South. It was a play/babysitting area where children could be left off while their parents, or other adult chaperone, shopped. The final idea was to use "eye-level signage" to attract kids and show parents how sensitive we were to their little darlings. The idea was developed using 180° Thinking, where we asked ourselves, "What's the worst way you would ever want to promote something to children?" The answers: You'd never want to hurt them in any way, maim them, poke the little bastards' eyes out.

Well, those less-than-pleasant thoughts led to "eye-level signage," cute little signs at the entrance and around the store that stood three feet high and pointed the way to the kiddie play area.*

John Zimmerman
President, o2ideas
Lobotomized 1995

* A moral to John Zimmerman's story is that you don't always need to know where your ideas come from.

> *180° Thinking isn't so much a place to take your finished thinking as it is a place to begin your exploration of new ideas.*

When your thinking takes you from soft to hard, "hard" is a new place to start your creative process. Could the bed be hard for your legs, but soft for your body and head? Might the bed be adjustable in its firmness, like my car seat? How about a bed that gets increasingly firmer in the moments before waking, a sort of gradual alarm clock that rouses you progressively instead of a screeching buzzer?

Is that final idea really 180° from how beds are currently manufactured? Well, no. But I arrived at it by starting in the opposite direction of conventional beds. As you can see, 180° can easily be the fresh, uncrowded territory where few thinkers tread. Might I have come up

Timeline of a great idea (continued)

Timeline of a lousy idea (continued)

"Wasn't yesterday bonus day? Hmm."

with this idea if I just decided to think of different ways to make beds better? Perhaps. I don't really know. I do know, however, that I did come up with this idea using 180° Thinking. And I did it quite quickly.

Many ideas appear to have been arrived at using 180° Thinking, whether or not the thinker knew he or she was using the technique: the shampoo bottle with the cap on the bottom, the sewing machine needle with the eye at the "wrong" end, the engine in the front of the car (it started in the back, contrary to what old Volkswagen lovers may like to think). There are also many ideas that have been developed using 180° Thinking *at some stage* in the process, even though the results of this opposite mentality may not be apparent in the final results.

What I like about 180° Thinking is how easy it is to get your mind out of the predictable patterns and into new places. Even if you just use it as a thinking blockbuster and the final idea bears no resemblance to the initial 180° thought, it doesn't matter as long as it shakes you from your predictable rational process and your final result is good.

BAD OR BETTER?

> *One of the greatest lessons to be learned from 180° Thinking is that we should not be so quick to discount our so-called bad ideas or mistakes.*

Don't discount an idea just because it is wrong according to traditional thinking or because it isn't what you intended. If an idea is totally against what you intended to do, or partially against it for that matter, don't be so quick to think it's not valid.

Some notable examples of accidental 180° Thinking that could be included in the innovation hall of fame: Vicks NyQuil, the cold remedy that was initially thought to be a failure because it put people to sleep, and Post-it notes, those little pieces of sticky paper that use that "bogus" adhesive whose molecules stick to only one surface. Failed products, according to the original intention, but accidentally brilliant.

Chapter 14, "Accidental Genius," gives you more examples of how being open to things you weren't looking for is an important part of creativeness.

How to Use 180° Thinking

Try it. You can't do wrong wrong.

Here's how to use 180° Thinking against a challenge or opportunity that you face:

Step 1. Identify some of the directions of thought that are typically used when thinking through such a situation.

Step 2. Push your thinking in the opposite direction. If you're working in a realm where you can isolate very definable traits or characteristics, sometimes it's helpful to write down those attributes, then next to each one write down the "untribute" (as I call it).

For example: Cold/hot. Big/small. Open/shut. Yes, there are some attributes that are not so easy to reverse, like *oat-flavored, rectangular,* or *French.* In cases like that, just think "not oat-flavored," "not rectangular," "not French."

Step 3. Now that you've identified the 180° possibilities, go with the flow. Work with the concept of "small," even though "big" is the accepted attribute. Work with "not rectangular" if what you're dealing with is rectangular. If not rectangular, then what? Round? Oval? Triangular? Shaped like the continental United States? It's that easy.

So Easy My Dog Can Do It

A few years ago my black Lab, Millie, showed me just how easy 180° Thinking can be. When invited to go for a ride in my new two-door convertible, Millie was faced with the challenge of getting her rather wide frame through the narrow opening that led to the backseat. Her solution? She aimed her ample body in the opposite direction and jumped on the back of the front seat, only to propel herself again in the opposite direction toward the backseat. This then became her everyday method of getting into the backseat of that car. Of course, this led to another creative challenge—protecting the fine leather on the back of my front seat from the marks left by her claws of steel. I have no doubt a solution will be found. Millie assures me she's working on it. (See creative problem solving cycle on page 57 in Chapter 3.)

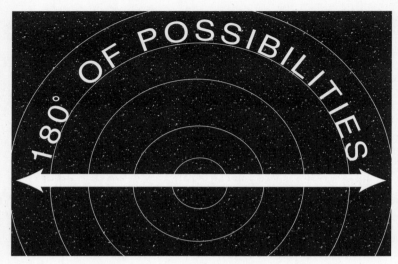

When you reestablish your base point 180° from conventional thinking, you not only have a new starting place for your thinking, but also a full 180° of territory to consider.

What's the Pressure?

The brakes on a train operate by air pressure. But the air pressure is not used in the way it was originally intended. It's used exactly the opposite way. You see, the first air brakes on trains were designed to operate as follows: Someone who wanted to stop the train would pull a certain lever, air pressure would trigger the brakes, and the train would stop. Problem was, the hoses that were used to channel this pressurized air were made of rubber, which erodes, wears out, and can be delectable to certain rodents. As holes developed in the rubber hoses, when the air brakes were triggered . . . well, you can probably figure out the unsatisfactory result.

The solution to this alarming problem was to reverse the thinking that produced air brakes in the first place. The improved method of stopping trains still used air pressure, but the air pressure was used to keep the brakes *off*. To stop the train, instead of using *pressurized* air to close the brakes, air was *released* to close the brakes. A 180° solution, if ever I saw one.

Oh, by the way, they still used the same type of rubber hoses to channel the air, but now if the rubber is compromised in any way, the brakes simply activate and stop the train. Yes, this could be a problem to deal with. But nowhere near as serious a problem as having no brakes when you need them.

INSPIRED BY 180° HEAT

Lyricist Sammy Cahn, one of the most prolific songwriters of the twentieth century, with standards such as "Carolina in the Morning," "High Hopes," and "All the Way" to his credit, tells a story about how he and his songwriting partner Jule Styne were inspired to write a song using 180° Thinking. It seems they had just exited a Hollywood producer's office with an assignment to write a song for an upcoming Bing Crosby movie. As they were going from the air-conditioned sanctuary of the office out into the 100+° heat on the steaming sidewalk, one of this famous writing duo suggested, "Let's go to the beach to write the song." Whereupon his partner is reputed to have suggested, "What do you say we just write a cool song?"

The result of this hot-weather-inspired effort was the classic holiday song, "Let It Snow! Let It Snow! Let It Snow!"

Timeline of a great idea (continued)

Timeline of a lousy idea (continued)

Bell-bottoms came back. Maybe there's hope for your idea yet.

Cheat Notes for Chapter 8: 180° Thinking

- *If you want to find new ideas, you have to look in a different place; 180° is "totally" different thinking.*

- *180° Thinking easily takes your mind out of the predictable patterns that bring you to the same place by forcing you to ignore all of the preconceptions in any category of thinking.*

- *Direct your thought process in the exact opposite direction of where conventional wisdom would suggest you go.*

- *If conventional wisdom says "soft," think "hard." If conventional wisdom says "warm," think "cold."*

- *If an attribute doesn't have an easily defined opposite, use the negative (e.g., for "rectangular," think "not rectangular").*

- *Even if you don't find an answer at 180°, you have a new place to start your creative process.*

- *Oh, by the way, did you understand "tnereffid" in the chapter title? It's "different" spelled backward.*

Intergalactic Thinking

Or, Why Think Outside the Box When You Can Think Outside the Galaxy?

We hear a lot these days about thinking *outside the box*. So much so that I'm tired of the term. So tired in fact that I'm going to give you a different, better term to use. But first we need to put the box in its final resting place.

The Nine-Dot Test

Solve this problem: Using only four straight lines, connect all nine dots without ever taking your pen off the paper.

● ● ●

● ● ●

● ● ●

This is where the expression "Thinking outside the box" comes from. Most people limit themselves to the area defined by the nine dots, in which case the puzzle cannot be solved. But as soon as you "think outside the box," it's much easier. The solution is located on page 257 if you haven't figured it out already.

WHAT IS THE BOX, ANYWAY? AND WHY DO WE NEED TO THINK OUTSIDE IT?

In most areas of thought, the box is simply what's been done, the tried-and-true traditional thinking, the comfort zone. Basically, it's what you already know — "the known," as discussed earlier, where your mind too often gets trapped.

Why do you need to think outside the box?

> *Outside the box is where the future will be created.*

It's where all the solutions to all the real problems will be found (see Chapter 2, "Creativity = Problem Solving").

How This Innocent Little Square Limits Creativity

Name something that you know about your field. Name anything. (For example, if you fish, you might name fishing net.) Using the writing instrument of your choice, place a dot anywhere inside the center box below to represent a bit of data that is in your daily realm of thought.

Now name something else you know about your field. Anything. Again, put a dot in the center box below to represent another bit of data you know.

You could go on for hours, making dots in your box, each one representing different specks of data about your field. If you did continue, completely exhausting your knowledge base, your box might end up looking something like the illustration on the top of the next page.

Now name something that has *nothing* to do with your field. Anything. How about the forty-first vice president of the United States? If Walter Mondale isn't already one of the bits of data inside your box, use your favorite writing instrument to put a dot

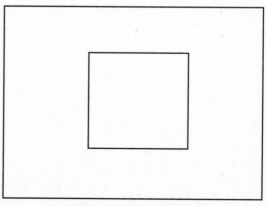

The easiest worksheet you'll ever do.

outside the center box here to represent this bit of data that has nothing to do with your field.

Name something else that has nothing to do with your field. Anything. Again, put a dot outside the center box representing that disjointed bit of data.

If you wanted to take the time to record every bit of data that you know that has nothing to do with your field, you'd do a pretty good job cluttering the void outside your box, which then might look something like what you see here on the right.

Everything you know that has nothing to do with your business is outside the box. As is everything you don't know,

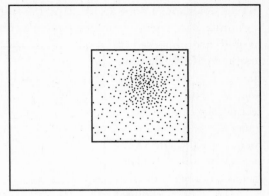

Inside the box.

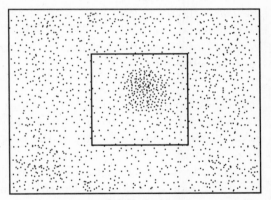

Outside the box.

along with everything no one knows yet. See where we're headed? Who says you don't think outside the box? You do it every day when you're not thinking about the things in your field.

THINKING OUTSIDE YOUR GALAXY

Take away the box and what do you have? See the next page. With a little imagination, it kind of looks like a galaxy in outer space. Why think outside the box when you can think outside the galaxy?

Imagine if you plotted the vast universe of ideas on an immense chart, with all the knowledge, data, and theories that have ever been entertained by the human mind since the beginning of time represented by stars. The chart might become an enormous star field, right?

Now imagine that these twinkling bits of data are arranged according to their relevance to one another. All the stars that have something to do with music are clustered in one galaxy of thought. All the ideas relating to golf are clustered in another galaxy. Banking data in yet another galaxy. Data relating to technology in its own galaxy. And so on and so forth for each and every group of related ideas. Each of these distinct clusters of thought would indeed look like the star galaxies in our vast physical universe.

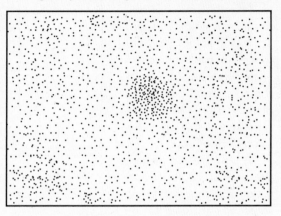

Well, one can argue that our universe of thought is quite similar to the realm of celestial bodies.

How Do Different Galaxies of Thought Relate?

As an example, let's see how a stockbroker might look at her or his galaxy in the context of some of the other galaxies in this universe we've created.

Let's start with the music galaxy. Does music have anything to do with the brokerage business? Doesn't seem to be closely related, does it? But let's push it a bit. Do brokerage firms play music in the office? Sure, some do. Are some of the stocks handled by some brokerage firms somehow related to music? Well, sure. Are some of the clients handled by stockbrokers involved in music? Of course, all kinds of people in music-related fields buy stocks. People who work at radio stations, people who make, sell, buy, or use records or musical instruments or sheet music or stereo equipment. There must be millions of people. So music is not squarely related to the brokerage business, but it's not unrelated, either.

Let's keep going.

How about the banking galaxy? Does anything in this galaxy have anything to do with the stock brokerage business? Absolutely. I'll bet if you think hard enough you might find hundreds or even thousands of bits of data. Gee, these distinct galaxies are seeming less and less distinct every minute.

How about the golf galaxy? What does that have to do with the bro-

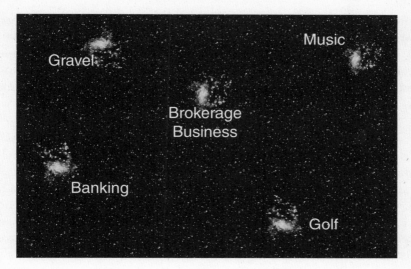

kerage business? Plenty. Isn't a lot of business conducted on the golf course? Aren't country clubs good places to wine and dine clients?

Let's look to this galaxy of thought for ways to improve the brokerage business. Don't you use different tools to attack different shots in golf? Your driver, fairway woods, irons of different denominations, wedges, putter, and so on. Do you have different tools and weapons when dealing with different situations in the brokerage business (telephone, e-mail, regular mail, cold calling, networking, etc.)? Are some golfers better at their short game than others and vice versa? Do players with opposite strengths make good partners in competitions such as best ball and scramble? Wouldn't John Daly with his long game off the tee make a great partner for Brad Faxon with his deadly putter in a best-ball round of a Ryder Cup tournament? Should some brokers divide and conquer to exploit their strengths? This could be a viable business strategy for the right brokerage team.

Fresh Start
This is how fresh ideas are often found. I call it Intergalactic Thinking. Simply going to seemingly unrelated galaxies that have nothing to do with our box of choice opens us up to whole new realms of creative possibilities.

Playing in Gravel
Let's go to the gravel galaxy now and really have some fun. What do you know about the gravel business? This industry underwent dramatic

improvement a few years ago, thanks to some very impressive Intergalactic Thinking.

The gravel business has been revolutionized in the past decade, thanks to a bit of data from another galaxy shown in our earlier illustration. Can you guess what it is? I'll give you a hint: It's in the banking galaxy.

Do you give up?

Well, believe it or not it's the ATM. At leading-edge gravel pits today, rather than pulling in and asking the guy with the shovel to help you load your truck with the haul of the day, you simply enter a weigh station, insert your ATM-like card into the ATM-like machine, and designate what kind of a withdrawal you want to make (pea stone, crushed rock, topsoil, whatever). Then you pull up to the chutes, load your vehicle, get weighed automatically, grab your receipt, and leave. The ATM technology is the latest thing in the gravel industry, and it is dramatically changing the way this field does business.

Somebody thought outside the box. In Intergalactic Thinking terms, they simply took a bit of data from outside their box, thus redefining the box forever. In this case, it may have happened on a trip to the bank. Probably a bank that some individual had been going to for years. But one day—*bingo!*—a brainstorm occurred.

Or maybe it didn't happen at the bank. Maybe someone just *thought* about an ATM when he or she was thinking through solutions to a problem. It happens.

It happens on your best days, effortlessly, when you get what we often call "inspired" by something. You know the feeling. You're looking at a beautiful sunset when, out of nowhere, a great idea hits you. Did the idea really come out of nowhere, or did you ask the question early, as we discussed in Chapter 6, and create an open-ended possibility in your mind?

CREATIVITY ON DEMAND

It may not matter how or why it happens, but the point is that ideas do come from unusual places quite often.

> *You don't have to wait for an inspiring sunset; you can make ideas happen, on cue, with little effort.*

You can perform a Do-It-Yourself Lobotomy whenever you want.

Just lobotomize the place in your mind where you normally think through a problem. You do that when you leave the known and go to some galaxy of thought that has nothing to do with your issue. This intergalactic mind travel disengages your rational mind—that predictable, boring thought maker that tosses around the same data over and over again—thus leaving you open to many more possibilities.

❧✦❧

A SUITCASE HISTORY OF INTERGALACTIC THINKING

I was sitting down with a high-level executive at one of the major luggage companies a few years ago. He asked me how Intergalactic Thinking might work on product design in his company. I asked him to go to the "farming" galaxy and name five things that had something to do with a farm. He named "pig," "fence," "tractor," "hoe," and "silo." Since I knew the routine, as he said each word I simultaneously let the concepts push me in different places relative to luggage design. I kept the thought process to myself.

"Tractor"? How about big wheels on the back, small wheels on the front of really large bags? Is that a good idea? I don't know. Then how about "pig"? Okay, maybe a corkscrew type of handle. That's stupid. ("Hey, don't judge!") Let's try "silo." A thought immediately popped into my mind. (Of course, all this happened in about five seconds. I do this kind of thinking all the time. It's second nature. See page 135.)

"That's it! Silos are used to store grains for the winter, so the livestock doesn't starve, right?" He looked at me strangely. "Do you make big boxes for off-season storage of clothing?" I asked. "Why, no we don't," was the luggage executive's reply. "Then I think you should consider getting into that business. People probably buy some no-name boxes for off-season clothes storage. Put your highly recognized name on that box, and it has instant brand equity, credibility, and added value."

The executive thought about it. He had the tooling, materials, suppliers, and distribution network—everything it takes to be in the off-season storage-container business. But he hadn't had the idea until we went looking in a foreign galaxy.

❖

INTERGALACTIC PROBLEM SOLVING

When do you need to think outside the galaxy? When you don't know the solution (which really should be all the time, because even when you think you know the solution, how do you know it's the best solution?).

When do you ordinarily *not* have a solution? When you encounter problems you've never faced before. We already established in Chapter 2 that there are basically two ways to solve a problem: Find solutions or create solutions. And where do you find things? In the known, or your "home galaxy."

When we can't find a solution, we are then forced to create solutions. Problems force us to stretch to a place outside our limited known; that's why we call it *creative* problem solving.

Since most people do consider *finding* solutions in the known to be a type of problem solving in addition to *creating* solutions, let's go with those two alternatives and see how this all ties together in the concept Intergalactic Thinking.

The Problem-Solving Spectrum

Let's look at what I call the problem-solving spectrum, because most of the time it isn't really a black-and-white issue of finding versus creating. Except for the old dyed-in-the-wool, tried-and-true ideas, virtually every idea has some components of both old and new thought.

When you can find a solution in your direct experience—that is, in your personal galaxy—you're at the less original thinking end of the spectrum.

But suppose you've never encountered this problem before (thus you have no direct experience), but you know someone who has been

The Problem-Solving Spectrum

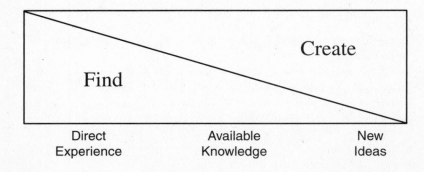

| Direct Experience | Available Knowledge | New Ideas |

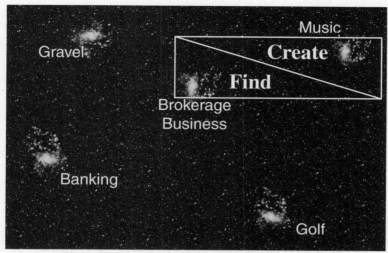

We tend to find ideas in our own galaxies, never thinking
to go elsewhere to "find" creative ideas.

there, or you find out through a little research what knowledge does exist. Then you're in the midrange of the spectrum. You take some known, put your own spin on it, and you have a somewhat original solution.

Now, let's take the far-right extreme. Let's say no one has ever faced this problem in this way before. There is virtually no knowledge, direct or otherwise, to draw upon. Then you have no choice but to create a solution.

Let's see how this all plays out intergalactically.

You tend to *find* in your home galaxy. And you tend to *create* outside your galaxy, what you may see as the unknown. But is it really unknown? Not in the least. Sure, it's beyond your home galaxy, but didn't we just discover that we know a great many things beyond our own private galaxy, outside our own box? If you think about it, it isn't truly a case of finding and creating, after all. We don't really create new ideas; we just find them outside our own galaxy.

So, you see, technically you can't be totally creative.

> *Scientists have been telling us for years that you can't really create anything.*

The Great Unknown. Oh, really?

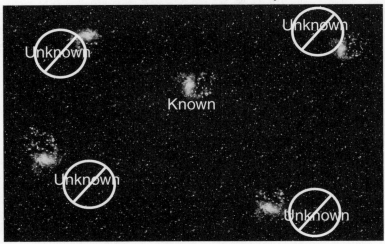

We tend to think of the area outside our home galaxy as the great unknown. But we do know a great deal that can be great starting places for creative exploration. It's not that the data relating to golf, music, banking, and gravel are unknown. We just think of it as inappropriate data for the solution mix. Or we don't think of it at all. But we're overlooking a great resource for creative inspiration.

Scientists used to say we can't create anything in the physical realm, we just transform energy and matter, until they discovered that matter is energy. So we don't create; we transfer energy. The same is true in the conceptual realm. New ideas are not really created; they're old ideas transformed. The only question is do we find the answer inside or outside the box. Traditional thinking or Intergalactic Thinking.

Intergalactic Thinking as a Conscious Creative Thinking Tool
You can practice Intergalactic Thinking in different ways. There's the strict, disciplined way used in both groupthink and when you're on your own. Then there's the method of simply being open to new ideas from any realm.

The most highly realized creative thinkers are usually people who can draw inspiration from almost anything almost anytime. Some of the greatest thinkers of all time were people who did not limit their thinking to the relatively small "atmospheric influence" of their own area of expertise. These Intergalactic Thinkers reached many of the greatest creative achievements of all time as a result of their intentional or unwitting use of data from a totally unrelated galaxy of thought to provoke a creative spark. (In Chapter 18, we talk about these hyper-creative types, whom I call *dreamers,* along with other creative personality types.)

❧❖❧

INTERGALACTIC THINKING IN EVERYDAY LIFE

Electrical engineer Philo Farnsworth, the man who made *the* breakthrough in the development of television, is said to have found his inspiration while he was tilling a potato field. Row by row, Farnsworth maneuvered his horse-drawn harrow back and forth, suddenly realizing that an electron beam could scan images the same way, back and forth, on a picture screen.

A number of years ago I was about to develop a TV campaign for a small breakfast cereal company. As I sat in on the preliminary meeting with the client, the media pros from my agency were telling the client that the best way to reach cereal consumers was morning TV. "TV?" the client said incredulously. "I can't even afford radio." That gave me the idea of doing a radio commercial on TV, which was much more economical to produce and helped drive home one of the main points of the commercial: Because we don't spend big bucks on advertising, we pass the savings on to you.

Rocker Patti Smith tells a story of how she was inspired to write a song about helicopters in Vietnam when she looked up in a recording studio and saw ceiling fans spinning their whirlybird-like rotors.

You can make lightning strike.

You don't have to wait until you're plowing a field or watching an industrial fan. You need not physically travel to another place to be struck by inspiration in this way. Did Philo Farnsworth have to be in a potato field to have been inspired by a potato field? No. He only had to think of that back and forth movement of a tractor to come up with his revolutionary idea. He could have gotten the same inspiration by reading a book line by line, by knitting a sweater row by row, or just by *thinking about* farming, reading, or knitting.

━━━━━━━━━━━❖━━━━━━━━━━━

What follows is the strict, disciplined way to use Intergalactic Thinking. It's the method I use in leading group brainstorming sessions and in coaching people at my Creativity Workshops. I suggest that you use this most disciplined process early on. As you begin to see the potential of this method, you'll use it often and become really good at it.

Here's how it works. Simply think of a galaxy of thought outside your everyday realm. I usually suggest people choose a galaxy that's fairly familiar, one very unrelated to their line of work, and one with many, many data points. I love using galaxies such as "the farm," "the ocean," or "the circus." I don't like galaxies with relatively few data points—like backgammon, taxidermy, or Russian musical instruments.

Start by picking a few data points in the galaxy of choice. If it's the ocean, you might choose "sand," "starfish," "boats," and "wind." Then, just try to connect these seemingly unconnected concepts to the problem at hand.

⇥◈⇤

How Intergalactic Thinking Works

Demonstration exercise: Working with a group trying to find ways to make better beds, we found many ideas in the ocean, so to speak.

One team thought up a bed shaped like a boat. Who uses the corners of beds anyway? We have square-shaped beds only because that's the way it has been done for years, starting with rope-strung bed frames. Do we need to use that shape today? Is it the best shape? Or is it just traditional thinking so entrenched that we can't envision any other way to shape a bed even if there is a better way? Sure, the entire sheeting and blanket industry is standardized around that rectangle shape, but does that mean it's the only way? Yeah, a boat-shaped bed might sound silly, even stupid, by conventional standards. Most new ideas do sound odd. Many are laughed at. And in many cases, real improvements don't happen, not because there are no new ideas, but because people can't fathom the new ideas (see "Stop Making Sense," page 155).

Another team thought up a bed that makes itself. They started with the concept of wind: Put a big fan at the end of the bed, then just let it blow the covers back into place. Practical? Well, don't be too judgmental. This team wasn't. They didn't kill this seemingly far-fetched idea. Quite the contrary. Instead they asked, "How do we make this thing work?" They came up with a contraption not unlike the mechanism that folds shirts at the laundry. Then they simplified it, using lines and pulleys. No, it still hasn't made it to perfection (no idea has), but it's a step in the right direction—an idea conceived using Intergalactic Thinking.

❖

Caution: Don't make Intergalactic Thinking too much of an intellectual exercise. For example, I've seen some novices listing dozens of data points from the city galaxy, stuff like "skyscrapers," "subways," "neon lights," and on and on, then waiting for something to happen. It doesn't work that way. Find only a few data points from the foreign galaxy. Anything to jog the mind out of the obvious galaxy. Then push for something to connect. Don't make it a drill in linear thinking. Don't rely on logic. Just focus on an unrelated piece of data and find a way to connect it to the problem. Ideas will come. It doesn't matter if the ideas seem crazy or stupid at first. Don't resist them. Find the brilliance. There's brilliance in almost anything.

I use Intergalactic Thinking in group brainstorming sessions almost every week and continue to be amazed at how effective it is in jumpstarting the creative process. When some people first try this, they feel like space shots. "This is crazy." "This is weird." "Beam me up, Scotty." But stay with it. Before you know it, this alien process becomes quite natural, and you've ramped up your ability to think creatively on demand. Pretty powerful stuff.

"Headhunter is calling.
  I smell a job offer."

Timeline of a great idea (continued) →

Timeline of a lousy idea (continued) →

Cheat Notes for Chapter 9:
Intergalactic Thinking

- *Outside the box is where the future will be created and where all solutions to all real problems are found.*

- *Everything you know that has nothing to do with your business is outside the box.*

- *Intergalactic thinking disengages your rational mind—that predictable, boring thought maker that tosses around the same data over and over again.*

- *Simply going to seemingly unrelated galaxies of thought that have nothing to do with your home galaxy opens up whole new realms of creative possibilities.*

- *Just focus on an unrelated piece of data and find a way to connect it to the problem. Don't make it a drill in linear thinking. Don't rely on logic.*

- *Don't resist ideas that seem crazy or stupid. Find the brilliance; there's brilliance in almost anything.*

Collaborate with Genius

The next Do-It-Yourself Lobotomy tool is a technique I call Collaborate with Genius™. This is a variation on Intergalactic Thinking, but rather than going to a galaxy of thought outside the area that you're working in, you instead go to a mind other than your own. You shouldn't collaborate with just anyone, however. Try to choose the assistance of a brilliant person. Because if you're going to collaborate with someone unbeknownst to them, why not collaborate with someone who can greatly enrich your idea pool?

How do you do this? Well, actually, you might simply say, "How would da Vinci approach this?" "How would Abraham Lincoln approach this?" "How would Bill Gates approach this?" "How would Bill Parcelles approach this?" The secret of Collaborating with Genius is to ask, "How would [name your genius] approach this?"

A Piece of Their Minds

This thinking tool is very easy to use. Simply choose a high-achieving individual and think.

> *Consult a football genius.* "Okay, Bill Parcells often worked on the lit-
> tle things that made the big things better. How can I work on the
> little things to make the big things better?"
>
> *Consult an inventor.* "Thomas Edison performed thousands of exper-
> iments with a filament before he got the filament that made for a
> better lightbulb. I could look at thousands of ways of doing
> this." Or you might be inspired by the fact that Edison napped

> ### The Lobotomy Files
>
> **May the Force Be with You**
>
> The Creative ForceField Analysis helps tear down every single barrier to creativity. It helps you better understand your culture and passions. It helped our company create and perpetuate a culture of creativity to make our thinking more inspired. The end product for our clients and ourselves is simply better thinking.
>
> Roy Spence
> President, GSD&M
> Lobotomized 1998

For more on the Creative ForceField see page 251.

many times a day; he had a bed in his laboratory because he felt that he always thought better when he was either falling asleep, waking up, or refreshed. You could use one of his habits. Collaborating with genius takes lots of forms.

You can be inspired by how someone else did things, or you can simply take one of the things they've done and use it as an Intergalactic data point. It really doesn't matter. What matters is that you get out of your own mind, because your own mind is the center of your universe, your known galaxy. Your own mind is where you keep crunching the same data all the time, not particularly fresh territory.

FOREIGN GENIUS IS BEST

Most people tend to go to high-achieving people in their own industry for inspiration or collaboration. Although that might be better than staying in your own mind, one of the problems here is that most people within your industry are emulating or being inspired by those same high-achieving but like-minded people. This doesn't necessarily add an advantage, and in many ways it allows you to stay too entrenched in your own galaxy of thought.

How do we get in the habit of collaborating with genius? My laboratory for the past 10 years has been the workshops that I run, and here's how we experiment with this tool under those conditions: I give the group a problem to solve using the mind of a high achiever. First you pick a high-achieving individual and write down 5 to 10 things that you know about that person. Here's how it works:

COLLABORATION WITH GENIUS EXAMPLE

Let's say you wanted to have inspiration from Abe Lincoln to help you solve a problem. First, you write down some traits of Abe Lincoln and go from there. For Honest Abe, you might write down the following list of traits:

Fair
Honest
Practical
Midwesterner
Tall

Now *practical* and *tall* are two very diverse things to write down. I remember a program in which I was asking people to improve passenger comfort in the coach section of an airplane and someone using "tall" came up with the idea of more headroom. It didn't seem practical because of all the lights and vents and buttons overhead. But what about lowering the seat? (Ask a Better Question can be used here as well.) Wouldn't that give us more headroom? Can we do this without reducing underseat storage space for the person behind? Do we need to rethink how the seat works? The material used? The cushioning system? The concept of "tall" led us to all these avenues of exploration and more. And isn't a seat-lowering mechanism already used in our cars?

It wasn't Abraham Lincoln's ideology or accomplishments, but rather his tallness, that led to an interesting solution. More typically, we're guided by philosophical issues, beliefs, or character traits.

"Hey, does that parking space have my name on it?"

Timeline of a great idea (continued) →

Timeline of a lousy idea (continued) →

Next time don't stop at your first idea.

Mental Gymnastics of Sorts

> *The greatest thinkers of all time have used other people's minds.*

Sir Isaac Newton, when talking about his own brilliance, said, "If I have great vision it is because I stand on the shoulders of giants." (Can you picture these geniuses balancing on one another's shoulders?)

If you follow the development of astronomy and physics and some of the sciences, you will see that Newton's work built upon Copernicus's, Einstein's work built upon Newton's, and Stephen Hawking's work built upon Einstein's. All these were within one category, but you can also, of course, be inspired by people outside your category.

In the music business, the early Stones hung around with the Beatles, and their first hit was written by the Beatles. Pete Townshend was inspired by Jimi Hendrix's opening at a club in London and, if you believe some of the stories, a little envious of Hendrix's capabilities.

Birds of Different Feathers

In many areas we see high-achieving people just hanging out with other high-achieving people. You've probably seen some of the famous photographs at the beginning of the twentieth century with Thomas Edison and George Eastman (of photography fame) posing with Harvey Firestone and Henry Ford. These were all brilliant men of their time in different areas of endeavor who associated with each other to borrow each other's brilliance and to stimulate each other's thoughts.

In contemporary life, Steven Spielberg hangs around with some of the icons of Silicon Valley; they're not even in the same industry, which is an excellent way to germinate ideas, as we discussed earlier.

In one of the original professional and personal development books, *Think and Grow Rich,* author Napoleon Hill speaks to a concept he calls a "Mastermind." He says that in order to be high achievers, we need to associate our thoughts with other high achievers, and they don't even have to be people we know. They can be dead people. They can even be people from fiction: Sherlock Holmes, Nancy Drew, Indiana Jones.

When I first started my ad agency years ago, I had a "psychic board of directors." Ad legend Bill Bernbach, who is deceased, was on that psychic board of directors. The Beatles were on my psychic board of directors. Jimi Hendrix was on my psychic board of directors. My previous boss was on my psychic board of directors. In fact, when I ran into him and told him, he said, "I haven't received any checks." And I replied, "Well, I've been sending you psychic wealth all these years."

❧❖❧

PLEASE, PLEASE COLLABORATE WITH ME

In the book *The Beatles Anthology* John Lennon talks about his development of the song "Please, Please Me." He says he was just trying to write a Roy Orbison song. (If you sing this classic Beatles song aloud or just hum the melody to yourself and you're at all familiar with 1960s rock 'n' roll, you'll recognize Roy Orbison's sound right away.) As Lennon was playing with the lyrics, there was something missing that he wanted to bring to the song. He found what he was looking for in, of all places, a Bing Crosby song with the words "please, please" in it.

Musicians and singers collaborate all the time when performing one another's material. Hendrix did Dylan's "All Along the Watchtower." Pavarotti, of course, does Puccini in many forms. Barbra Streisand, although she has written some wonderful material, has also collaborated with many great writers over the years, styling their songs with her unique touch. Rap artists have taken collaboration to an entirely new place with sampling.

You may recall a few years ago when the then three living Beatles collaborated with the deceased John Lennon by adding their tracks to his basement recordings of "Free as a Bird." I had to laugh at the minor uproar this recording caused. Many people took exception to the fab three's collaborative effort. California ex-governor Jerry Brown almost blew a head gasket over it. Did he not recognize how Lennon himself collaborated with people in the grave—Buddy Holly, for instance?

It's not just in music. I'd say it is impossible for anyone on this planet to get up in the morning and make it through a day without collaborating with some deceased soul. The question is, are you collaborating with geniuses or mere mortals? If you're doing it consciously, it's more likely to be the former.

———————— ❖ ————————

You can use the thoughts of other great people. You have the ability. All these thoughts become part of the public domain at a certain point in time.

Are you choosing to be guided by brilliant people, standing on the shoulders of giants, or are you standing on the shoulders of mental midgets, the dullards who do what's been done a thousand times before in your industry? If your source of inspiration is to watch wrestling on TV, I'm not convinced you're going to nourish your mind. High-achieving people constantly try to elevate their minds and continually strive to be inspired by one another. We discuss this at length toward the end of the book (Chapter 21) when I speak to biographies as some of the greatest creative thinking textbooks ever written.

Cheat Notes for Chapter 10:
Collaborate with Genius

- *Get out of your own mind where you keep crunching the same data all the time; it's not particularly fresh territory.*

- *Rather than going to a galaxy of thought outside of the area that you're working in, instead* go to a mind other than your own.

- *Don't collaborate with just anyone; seek the assistance of a brilliant person.*

- *You can be particularly inspired by people outside your category.*

- *The secret of Collaborating with Genius is to ask, "How would [fill in high-achieving individual of choice] approach this?"*

CHAPTER 11

Conceptual Solitaire

Here's a little exercise that I have developed to help people solve problems. I call it "Sentenced to Death." This exercise is ideal for people who work alone or who need to brainstorm alone. If group brainstorming is like the Friday night poker game, this is more like "Conceptual Solitaire™." It's simple. Try it now. Take a few minutes to complete this exercise, using a problem you are currently facing, before reading further. Use the worksheet on the next page.

Step 1.   Choose an issue to brainstorm solo. Preferably it is an issue you're currently facing, something that may have popped up this week or something you've been facing for years without a solution.

Step 2.   Write your problem on the top line of this worksheet. I suggest trying to get the problem down to 8 to 12 words. I also suggest the first sentence be a question.

Step 3.   On the second line write a second sentence that incorporates a key word or phrase from your first sentence. (The second sentence doesn't have to be a question.)

Step 4 and on.   Continue to rephrase the statement on each successive line, incorporating a new key word or phrase from each preceding sentence into the sentence immediately following.

Sentenced to Death Worksheet

_____

_____

_____

_____

_____

_____

_____

_____

_____

_____

_____

_____

_____

_____

_____

_____

_____

_____

_____

_____

_____

_____

What Happened?

When you continually reprocess a topic and push it in different directions, particularly if you do it quickly and succinctly, a number of things can happen:

- *You can solve the problem.* Just by throwing a great deal of concentrated energy against an issue you can actually force a solution.
- *You can make progress toward a solution even if you don't fully solve it.* The progress brings the ball farther down the field, even if it's not a touchdown, so that you might be able to solve it later.
- *You discover the real problem.* Many people who have used this process have told me it doesn't necessarily solve the problem they tackle, but sometimes, just as important, it helps them identify the problem behind the problem.
- *You realize the problem isn't a problem after all.* Or at least you find it's less of an issue than you thought.
- *Sometimes you gain or release responsibility.* Maybe claiming a problem that you think is someone else's fault causes you to see your own role in it. Maybe the process helps you release your responsibility, "Screw 'em. Let *them* deal with it."

In all cases you gain perspective.

> *The worst thing you can do is to just sit with a problem.*

Psychologist and author Wayne Dyer says, when you have a problem, "Do something." What? "Anything." Don't just sit with it. A former chairman of 3M, when put on the spot by the press about his company's penchant for "stumbling over" new ideas, is reputed to have said, "You can't stumble if you're not moving."

Cheat Notes for Chapter 11:
Conceptual Solitaire

- *Conceptual Solitaire is an ideal process for brainstorming by yourself.*

- *The worst thing you can do is to just sit with a problem.*

- *Throwing a great deal of concentrated energy against an issue can actually force a solution.*

- *Even if you don't find a solution, you will likely make progress, discover the real problem, or maybe release or accept responsibility.*

- *In any case, you're likely to find a fresh perspective.*

How to Put These Tools to Work

As promised in the beginning of Part III, here are some simple, easy-to-follow instructions about how to use these tools for optimal results.

USE THEM OR LOSE THEM

First, *use* your new thinking tools. As soon as you can, use them. When you put down this book, even before you finish it, use any one of your new thinking tools to deal with whatever problem, challenge or opportunity that comes your way (which means anytime, anywhere, because *everything* is a creative opportunity).

Have you ever taken a golf lesson, a tennis lesson, a piano lesson, or such? If you don't use the newly honed skills immediately, what happens? Let's say you wait a week before going to the practice range after taking a golf lesson. Do you know what happens? You've forgotten almost everything you learned. "Are my hands supposed to be above my shoulder on the backswing?" "Am I supposed to lead with my hip?" You're not sure, so you practice timidly at best, or you practice wrong at worst, putting yourself in an even deeper groove of improper mechanics. You're going to need three lessons to correct the effects of one misinterpreted lesson.

REPETITION DEVELOPS NEW HABITS

After you've used any one of these thinking tools and are happy with the results, use it again as soon as you can. On a golf course, if you hit the ball well, you can't lay down a new ball and try to replicate the swing while the memory is still fresh in your mind and in your body. At the practice range, that's exactly what you do to find a good groove. It's the same with these thinking tools. Don't just practice; practice perfectly.

If the tool doesn't feel quite right when you first use it, stick with it a while. You're working against years of old habits and stale patterns of thought. It will take some time before these new methods become second nature. But it will happen. With repetition, that is.

BACK TO SCHOOL

Let's say that one of these tools feels somewhat awkward as you're using it or the results are not satisfactory. Then maybe you need to go back to school. I've made it very easy for you in this book, thanks to the "cheat notes" at the end of each chapter.

When you have a need to review, I suggest you check out the cheat notes first. If they don't jog your memory sufficiently, simply reread the entire chapter, or at least skim through it. Again, you're working against *years* of old thinking habits. Although many people experience huge changes in their thinking abilities overnight with these tools, for others it takes a little longer. Sometimes, the first few times you use the tools they work quite well, but later they start feeling less effective. Always go back to the cheat notes or reread the appropriate chapter.

USE ANOTHER TOOL

Here's another way to deal with any difficulty you may have in learning or using any of these tools. Let's say you're having some trouble with Ask a Better Question (and this goes for a beginner or even a veteran like me): *Use a different tool.* Don't try to fix a tool that doesn't seem to be working. Don't panic. Just use another tool. Perhaps you should try Intergalactic Thinking for a while. These tools differ from dental tools or plumbing tools in that your plumber can't just pick up a monkey wrench when the soldering iron is broken. But these thinking tools are often quite interchangeable.

Then there are days when you just accept that one tool is going to work better for you than another. Sometimes when I'm on the golf course, my 9-iron just isn't working, but what do you know? My putter helps make up the slack. That's why you have more than one club in your golf bag. That's why I have developed many types of Do-It-Yourself Lobotomy tools.

IS IT THE TOOL OR THE WORKER?

If you're having an impossible time coming up with a fresh idea using this or that tool, or even if you're coming up dry using all of the tools, ask yourself, "Is it the tools, or is it me?"

Think about it. The whole reason I developed these tools is because people become attached to old ideas, so they often need strong levers to pry their minds off that old stuck place.

I have worked with companies where some people walked into the room saying, "There's no way to do this better." The stuck person goes through the motions and participates in the brainstorming session, seemingly involved just like everyone else. But if in the end this naysayer doesn't come up with any new ideas, is it because the tools didn't work or because this person simply wasn't open to the new ideas that presented themselves during the thinking process? A more open, less detached coworker gives it a shot and is very successful. You tell me, is it the tool or the worker?

Fortunately, you are not that kind of person. How do I know this? Because you're reading this book.

MY GUARANTEE

I offer a guarantee at my workshops. I will offer it here. If you don't use any of these tools, I guarantee they will not work.

> *Like the tools in my basement, if I don't use these thinking tools they get rusty.*

Conversely, the more you use these tools, the more effective they become. I might even say they are self-sharpening tools: The more you use them, the sharper you become.

People often ask me if I use these tools. Well, to be honest with you, I rarely do anymore.

WHY I DON'T USE THESE TOOLS

These methods of thinking have become second nature to me. Because I have used them so regularly for so many years, I usually think this way without using them consciously. I almost always ask better questions, not always to the applause of my wife and others around me. I love looking at many possible solutions to any given problem, and I love thinking of lots of ideas very quickly, so 100 MPH Thinking as a formal tool is no longer necessary for me. I also love to find inspiration for ideas in out-of-the-way places, which makes Intergalactic Thinking unnecessary in its codified form. As for 180° Thinking . . . hey, I'm a child of the '60s, I've always been counter to everything.

But when I'm stuck, when a fresh idea doesn't come to me easily, BAM! That's when I take one of these powerful tools out of my thinking arsenal and blow the problem away.

Okay, I admit it. I *do* use these tools. On the bad days I do. But because I live them . . . well . . . I simply don't need to use them consciously and purposefully as much. And if you use them regularly, you won't have to use them so intentionally, either.

CONSCIOUSNESS LEADS TO UNCONSCIOUSNESS

You know what they say about an athlete when he or she just can't miss? When a basketball player can't miss a shot, they say he is *unconscious*. When a tennis player puts every ball in just the perfect spot, they say she is *unconscious*. Well, that is the endgame of all this consciousness we're trying to get you to embrace with these concepts and practices: When you really, really get it all down pat, you won't have to think about it at all.

If you feel like reading a bit more, just remember to use the tools as soon as you can. The remainder of this book is designed to help add

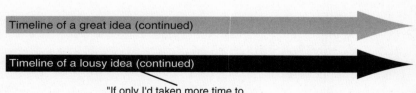

Timeline of a great idea (continued)

Timeline of a lousy idea (continued)

"If only I'd taken more time to
think of a few more ideas."

dimension to the tools you've just learned. Like the fundamentals in Part II that preceded the tools in Part III, the final section, on dimensionalizing, offers much helpful information and many additional perspectives about creativeness in general and how to maximize yours.

Now, enough of the talk. Put this book down right now and go use one of your new Do-It-Yourself Lobotomy tools!

Cheat Notes for Chapter 12:
How to Put These Tools to Work

- *Use them or lose them. As with golf lessons or piano lessons, the learning fades fast.*

- *Repetition develops new habits. The more you repeat, the deeper the new grooves.*

- *Refer to the Cheat Notes for a quick reference. (You can even make copies of the Cheat Notes pages and carry them as a "Creative Survival Kit.")*

- *If a particular tool doesn't seem to be working, don't panic. Just use another tool.*

- *If you don't use any of these tools, they will not work — guaranteed.*

- *The more you use the tools, the sharper they'll become and the sharper you'll become.*

Conventional wisdom says an athletic shoe should be lightweight and flexible.

Athletic shoes are lightweight and flexible, right? As a rookie copywriter I cut my teeth in the athletic shoe arena, and I can tell you I must have written "light and flexible" into a thousand different ads. But not often enough for my clients.

Well, a few years ago when I developed painful heel spurs, from who-knows-what physical activity, my podiatrist suggested I try a particular Nike training shoe that wasn't exactly light and was far from flexible. In fact, the shoe is damn heavy and downright rigid. After three weeks of using these Frankensteinian shoes my heel spurs stopped bothering me and I was back to working out.

Conventional thinking says "lightweight and flexible" is the way to go. 180° Thinking says, maybe not. Those creative designers at Nike decided to just not do it. For more heavy reading on 180° Thinking, go to Chapter 8.

How about an advanced athletic shoe that's heavy and stiff?

PART IV

Dimensionalizing Your New Creative Tools

In Parts I and II of this book we covered some of the fundamental aspects of creativity that I felt must be laid down as a foundation for the Do-It-Yourself Lobotomy thinking tools covered in Part III.

Here in Part IV, we touch upon a potpourri of other subjects. I've found, as a creative thinking coach, when these topics are more clearly understood they help students of creativeness make better use of the tools—the mechanics of the creative process—to help them become more fully realized creatively.

Part IV sheds light on simple aids to creativity such as *observation* and *jotting notes*. This material helps you better understand the nonrational aspect of creative ideas, especially the concepts in Chapter 14, "Accidental Genius," and Chapter 15, "Stop Making Sense." In Part IV we also cover practical topics such as selling your ideas, conducting brainstorming sessions, and managing others for greater creativity. In addition, we discuss the greatest barriers to creative realization and how to overcome them.

Some of this might sound theoretical, but I learned much of this in the laboratory of my profession, the workshops and brainstorming sessions I run almost weekly with real people in real business situations. I can assure you there is much practical knowledge to be gained in this section.

Aids to Creativity

Many people think that to be creative requires active participation in the creative process, actively thinking of new ideas. And in the end, yes, thinking of new ideas is a big part of creativity. But what stimulates creativity, what creates the canvas for creativity, is understanding where the need for creativity lies.

OBSERVATION

Of course, this is not an original concept; this is how Leonardo da Vinci thought about creativeness. He felt as though observation was the foundation of his creativeness. And if you study the life of da Vinci, you'll find that observation was key to many of his accomplishments. He looked at birds, observed, and wondered, "How do they fly?" He didn't know how they flew. But his wonderment led to some of the earliest thinking about the concept of manned flight.

I still don't know how birds fly, and I've observed birds a thousand times or more. But I've never observed them with a sense of wonder like da Vinci. Never observed and allowed myself to go to the place that I didn't know. Most of us observe and simply stop at what we know—"Oh, there are birds flying," as opposed to, "How do they do that?"

Da Vinci looked at fish and wondered, "How do they swim?" His wonderment there led to the thinking behind the development of the submarine.

> Observe. *Don't just take things at face value. Observe and wonder. "This is how it is. . . . How might it be done better?"*

Sometimes we're shaken into action by a big problem when we realize that what we're doing doesn't work. But it's the great minds (or it's us when we're thinking at our best) who, when faced with a situation that *does* work, still wonder how it might work better. That happens from observation.

I don't know about you, but when I think of observation I think of my eyes observing. Well, if observation as a concept is ill understood, the listening aspect of observation is even less understood.

LISTENING IS A GREAT CREATIVE SKILL

A number of years ago, I attended a communications workshop and learned something about conscious listening. We all think that we listen all day long. But let's say you're in a business meeting or a brainstorming session, listening to a speech, or listening to a voice-mail message, and someone's remark sends your mind immediately off on a tangent of how you might follow up or respond. If you're thinking of what your answer is going to be, *you aren't listening.* You may be missing the answer to your own question being discussed by the other individual. For example, in a lecture, you may not be getting everything you desire from the speaker because you're too busy going off on your own mental tangent.

Listening means being engaged with the speaker. And one aspect of listening that leads to tremendous ideation possibilities is the concept of *jotting,* which we'll discuss next. Whether you're in a dialogue with someone, watching a program on TV, sitting in a classroom, or attending a business meeting, jot down the thoughts that come into your mind while you're listening. Notice, I intentionally use the word *jot,* not *write down.* Just jot down the gist of the ideas that are coming into your mind; take yourself away from the active listening for just a brief moment and jot. Or, if you're more graphically inclined, sketch. Don't draw, *sketch.* Either way, briefly capture the gist of the idea that you have. And when you're done, you can go back to being an active listener. You can go back to hearing more, to observing more. Jot rather than taking the time to write things down.

The same thing is true in brainstorming, as we'll discuss on page 209. Often, when people have an idea during brainstorming, they start writing it down in detail, finding out what's wrong with it, and deciding how to make it happen. While they're in this state, what I call the *execution mode,* they're not in *sparking-of-ideas mode.* Our minds operate on many different planes, and I can assure you that the sparking-of-ideas mode is very different from the rational, linear, let's-prove-it-out, let's-think-it-through, let's-use-logic modes that we use when we're executing or just thinking through a problem. Jotting becomes an aid to creativeness because jotting allows you to observe and write down the gist of whatever ideas that come into your mind while remaining in ideation mode. All of which brings us to another aid to creativity.

Taking Notes

Many of the greatest thinkers of all time were great note takers because they recorded almost anything that came into their minds. Leonardo da Vinci was a great note taker, and to this day some of his manuscripts have survived. A number of years ago, I went to the Museum of Natural History in New York City when the codex of da Vinci notes owned by Bill Gates was touring the world. I don't know if you've seen any of da Vinci's notes, but he wrote his ideas down backward so people wouldn't steal them. And he could read them in a mirror. Talk about a brilliant thinker.

⇌❖⇋

You Just Blew $1 Billion

I know a lot of people think, "I don't need to take notes. If it's a brilliant idea I'll remember it." Well, I ask you, "How do you know? How do you know if you've forgotten it?" Did you have a billion-dollar idea last week that could have changed your life and changed the industry you work in and maybe earned you or your company a fortune? Maybe you've since forgotten it. How do you know? The good news is that we don't *know* what idiots we are when we don't write things down and lose brilliant ideas.

I know people think, "I'll never forget something really important." Oh, really? Tell me where you put your insurance documents at home. It's going to take you two hours to find those things, those really important things you put in just the perfect spot so you'll never forget where they are.

❖

Lee Iacocca is among many captains of industry who are noted for taking notes (bad pun noted). Jotting down the ideas that come into your mind is an aid to accomplishment no matter what field you're in. Random ideas are often the impetus for big breakthroughs, as we discussed in Chapter 9, "Intergalactic Thinking." But if you don't write down a random idea, you might lose the inspiration for a huge solution.

Many years ago, when I was new to the ad business, I did a campaign with Steve Allen, the great comedian/musician/philosopher. Although this was back in the 1970s, Steve Allen had a mini–cassette recorder in his top pocket, probably leading-edge technology at that time. During the shooting of TV commercials, at lunch, or on a plane, he would periodically pick up this little device and say something into it; he had people at his home base transcribing his notes and cataloging his thoughts.

There's a wonderful story Keith Richards tells about conceiving the riff that defines the song "Satisfaction," which many people think is one of the best rock 'n' roll songs of all time (number one in VH1's Best Rock 'n' Roll Songs of all Time Top 100). Keith woke up in the middle of the night with this riff in his head. He grabbed a little tape recorder and he hummed into it the melody of the eight notes. In the morning he noticed his tape recorder on his pillow and he said, "What's that?" He didn't even remember having conceived this riff and recording it. He picked up the tape recorder, rewound it, and he heard the now famous signature from "Satisfaction," followed by 45 minutes of snoring. If he hadn't recorded his idea, hadn't jotted it down electronically, he would have lost it forever.

Rick Pitino, one of the greatest basketball minds of all time,* in an interview with *Success* magazine, was asked, "What are your secrets of success?" And this basketball coach extraordinaire said that one of his top secrets of success is that he

> The strongest memory is weaker than the palest ink.
>
> Ancient Chinese proverb

writes everything down. The interviewer went on to ask why writing everything down was one of the coach's secrets to success. To which Pitino replied, "Because, if I don't write down important things, I might forget." We are all fallible in this regard.

---

*As I write this, Rick Pitino is between jobs, having left the Celtics. Many people who follow basketball might say that he was a monumental failure in his tenure with Boston's NBA franchise. But mark my words: Rick Pitino learned more in his bad experience with the Celtics than he learned from all his great experiences as a basketball coach. He will be back.

This is one of the foundational aspects of creative thinking: Write things down when you think of them. I suggest you jot down the gist and expand it a bit, just enough so you know what you mean by that little tidbit. If we don't surround it with quite enough meaning, sometimes our jotting becomes meaningless to us later on.

"Hey, they're hiring 15 new people, thanks to your new idea."

Timeline of a great idea (continued)

Timeline of a lousy idea (continued)

Cheat Notes for Chapter 13:
Aids to Creativity

- *Observe, but don't just take things at face value. Observe and wonder.*

- *Active listening means being engaged with the speaker.*

- *Quickly jot down the gist of the ideas that are coming into your mind; take yourself away from the active listening for just a brief moment and jot.*

- *Capture (write, record) any random idea you have when you think of it. If you don't, you might lose the inspiration for a huge solution.*

Accidental Genius

> *A big part of being a highly realized creative person is having an open mind and being able to recognize great ideas even when you aren't looking for them, perhaps even when they are the last thing you are looking for.*

New ideas come about almost entirely in one of two ways: (1) when someone thinks up a new idea and (2) when mistakes happen, that is, mistakes in action or mistakes of the mind. Most of this book is about the first method—purposefully coming up with fresh ideas. But being open to the gifts of what I call *accidental genius* is also a way to discover new things, and often the only effort it takes is being open to them when they present themselves. This is something that is much easier said than done for most people.

In the chapter about 180° Thinking, we talked about mistakes often leading to better results than what you had in mind when you went looking for a new idea or a solution to a problem. We cited Post-it notes and NyQuil as being two examples of unintentional 180° Thinking. These and thousands of other less purposefully discovered new ideas and new ways of thinking and doing could also be categorized as accidental genius. Here are a few other examples.

MELTDOWN OF AN OLD PARADIGM

The story of how the concept behind the microwave oven was "discovered" is a perfect example of accidental genius. It seems a certain scientist was working with microwaves in a laboratory, when he felt something warm and sticky in his pocket. His chocolate bar had changed viscosity thanks to the heat generated by the microwaves as they churned the nearby atoms into a minor riot of molecular proportions. And, thus, a new way of cooking was born.

DYLAN'S OPEN EAR

There's a story that rocker Al Cooper tells about some accidental genius that catapulted his career in the mid-1960s. Cooper had been an average guitar player and singer as one of the creative forces behind The Blues Project, one of the first American bands to bring blues to the rock audience. When he was invited to accompany Bob Dylan in recording *Highway 61 Revisited*, Dylan's first plugged-in recording, Cooper naturally brought his guitar to the session. During the recording of Dylan's classic, "Like a Rolling Stone," when the great guitar player Mike Bloomfield, also invited to the session, sat down to play, an accident of sorts occurred in the recording studio that led to an unexpected birth of genius.

Feeling a bit outclassed by Bloomfield's superior guitar playing, a self-conscious Cooper put down his own guitar and slid behind the electric organ, which he barely knew how to play, hoping he could blend in by simply throwing in a few chords occasionally.

After the first couple of takes, the recording engineer pulled Dylan into the listening suite and pointed out the strange sounds coming from Cooper trying to fake his way through the song on organ. Dylan, on hearing an organ played like he had never heard it played before, proceeded to ask the engineer to bring the instrument up in the mix, thus giving his first electric hit the unique organ sound that became its signature.

Cooper later went on to enjoy an illustrious career as an organist with a sound that was far from conventional. He then got offers to be a studio musician on the organ. Cooper credits the strange circumstances of that first recording session and Bob Dylan's open mind for discovering his accidental genius.

WHO'S THE DUMMY NOW?

One of the first TV spots I ever wrote had Steve Allen—comedian, musician, songwriter, philosopher, and all-around creative genius—

doing a comic bit with a ventriloquist dummy in his own likeness (don't ask) for a bank client. We recorded Allen's voice in advance for the dummy's lines, and during one of the early takes Allen stepped on his own line and proceeded to acknowledge the mistake with big eyes to the camera, in a broad "early live TV" kind of way. The director yelled "Cut" from off-camera, but Allen kept going, finishing the final lines and the scene. The camera operator, luckily, kept the film rolling. At the end of the scene Allen whispered to me, "That's the take we'll use."

The clueless director, trying to nail the script perfectly, went on to film a half dozen more takes. You can guess the end of the story. We went with the botched take. It was funnier; it gave Allen the gift of an accident to create something better than what was asked for; and, above all else, the commercial was very memorable and helped give a big boost to the advertiser's awareness levels. In the end, the only edit required was eliminating the closed-minded director's "Cut" from the audio.

THE CASE OF THE MISSING FOUR SECONDS

One of my last TV spots before leaving the ad business may not have been the most important commercial I ever did, nor was it for the biggest client, but it did give my art director partner, Holland Henton, and me the gift of yet another lesson in accidental genius.

This was a 15-second commercial for an ABC network affiliate promoting their *Roseanne* reruns during the early-fringe 5:00–6:00 P.M. time slot. It was one of a package of six spots, all starting off with a freeze-frame of the TV show with comedian Gilbert Gottfried as the voice-over saying something pithy or totally inane, as the case may be. Then the tape would roll for about eight seconds in each spot, featuring a clip from a rerun. At the end came a freeze-frame where the voice-over would return and the station's logo would appear.

In this particular commercial, the script for the head of the spot read, "How'd you like to come home to this every night at 5:30," spoken in Gottfried's patented sloppy, Brooklyn-accented scream. Then we were supposed to have a clip from the show showing Roseanne being the far-from-average average housewife in the title role. The problem was this: When edited, the chosen clip showing Roseanne running toward the camera hollering fell four seconds short. It seems the intern who had selected the initial batch of takes we considered using for the spot had forgotten to time all of the scenes. Now, if you're not in advertising, you may think, what's four seconds? If you are in advertising, you understand our dilemma. Four seconds is an eternity, especially in a 15-second commercial.

As I recall, the initial thought was to look at some of the takes we had passed over to find a replacement scene that could fill our four-second hole. But then someone with an open mind (I still can't recall who) said, "Hey, let's try slowing the footage down to fill the hole."

Well, let me tell you, the gods of creativity were smiling down on us this day. When we slowed down the tape, not only did we get to see Roseanne lumbering toward the camera in slow motion like a charging rhino on *Wild Kingdom,* a very funny sight, but, surprising all of us, the slowed-down sound track created an amazing effect. If you don't know anything about sound recording, slowing down a sound creates a lower pitch. I'm talking about a *much* lower pitch . . . like turning Tweety Bird into Lurch on *The Addams Family.* So now the charging-rhino housewife is sounding like lizards-turned-dinosaurs in a cheap Japanese horror flick.

Believe me when I tell you, this commercial was hilarious, and not only funny to a bunch of advertising executives who had just dodged a minor bullet, but to a much more demanding audience. You see, this innocent little low-budget local TV spot impressed some of the most savvy advertising professionals in the business that year, and they put this commercial into the winner's circle at the One Show Annual, one of the most prestigious, most difficult advertising competitions on the planet.

BO DOESN'T KNOW

Another commercial that benefited from some accidental genius was from Nike in the early 1990s. Most students of advertising remember the epic "Bo knows Diddley" spot created by Wieden + Kennedy for Nike's cross-trainer using cross-sport athlete Bo Jackson and rhythm-and-blues great Bo Diddley.

The commercial featured big-name athletes from various sports saying "Bo knows [insert appropriate sport]." Michael Jordan saying, "Bo knows basketball." Jim Everett saying, "Bo knows football." Joan Benoit, John McEnroe, Wayne Gretzky, and others exclaiming the athletic prowess of Bo Jackson. This introductory phrase was intercut with images of the versatile athlete playing the various appropriate sports, all to the rhythm of Diddley's signature hand-jive beat.

In the original commercial, the final scene shows Jackson trying quite unsuccessfully to play the guitar, with Diddley saying, "Bo, you don't know diddly."

Months after the original spot first ran, Nike aired an alternative version that had Bo Jackson playing a mean guitar throughout. This sequel spot ended with Bo Diddley saying, "Bo, I guess you do know diddly."

When I was judging the New York Art Directors Club awards competition later that year I asked one of the campaign's creators, David Jenkins, if they had planned to cut two versions of the commercial all along. He confessed that the creative team played almost no role in the generation of the second spot. It seems that the film editor was inspired by an outtake where Bo Diddley uttered the "I guess you do know diddly" line. The technician simply edited 30 seconds of footage of Bo Jackson at the guitar meshed deftly with the music track to give the illusion he could actually play the instrument, then cut the Bo Diddley outtake onto the end.

In this case, the editor's open-mindedness grasped the potential of the mistake in the original shooting. Additionally, it took the open-mindedness of the creative team and client to go with the unsolicited alternative.

RAIDERS OF A NEARLY LOST SCENE

If you remember the original Indiana Jones movie, *Raiders of the Lost Ark*, you might recall a very funny scene in the public marketplace where our hero shoots the big, ominous sword-wielding nemesis. To refresh your memory, the crowd parts as the imposing villain taunts protagonist Indy with an impressive series of swooshing-blade moves. The Harrison Ford character, holding his patented bullwhip, sums up his immense challenge, then makes a face, puts the whip in his other hand, pulls out a gun, and shoots the bad boy dead.

It was a moment of huge yuks in the film.

Well, did you know that the scene wasn't written that way? It seems our star, Ford, was feeling under the weather during that day of filming, so rather than trying to manage his way through an exhausting physical scene, he improvised and pulled out the pistol, surprising even director Spielberg.

Again, accidental genius, the unplanned guest, saves the day.

PLANNING IS OVERRATED

A number of years ago I read a piece in the *Wall Street Journal* that talked about the dangers of adhering too closely to a plan. The point of the article was this:

> *If you stick slavishly to what you plan to do you might miss better opportunities that pop up along the way.*

In *Bottom Up Marketing*, Al Ries and Jack Trout speak of strategic planning as being overrated as well. These two gentlemen, who have guided the marketing world for years with best-sellers such as *Positioning* and *Marketing Warfare*, caution us not to let steadfast adherence to a strategy prevent us from finding winning tactics along the way. They point out that strategy is often done by making certain assumptions, but if those assumptions don't hold true in the face of reality, then we're better off being open to the tactics that will work at that time, whether they fit with the strategy or not.

As a consultant to ad agencies, I often hear clients or people in account service complain that the ads the creative people are coming up with are not "on strategy." Having creative-directed about 100 of these sometimes impulsive animals over the years, I can certainly see how their lack of discipline occasionally derails the strategic process. At the same time (and maybe this is because I was one of those derailing creative types for so many years), I can understand that in some of those cases the creative process had the gift of accidental genius. I know because I have been there that sometimes you actually find a better way during the heat of the battle. The foxhole is a lot closer to reality than the insular war room.

OPEN YOUR MIND

So remember this, when you engage in the creative process and something comes up that you didn't intend, don't be so quick to discount it as being wrong. It just might be better than what you intended.

And, to those in management, if your charges come back to you with something you didn't ask for, before you dismiss it out of hand, take a good look at this new idea. It just might be better than the idea you were looking for in the first place. It could be accidental genius riding a white horse to the rescue, and maybe you don't want to look this gift horse in the mouth.

Timeline of a great idea (continued)

Timeline of a lousy idea (continued)

"Hey, how's it going?"   "Oh, sorry."

Cheat Notes for Chapter 14:
Accidental Genius

- A big part of being a highly realized creative person is having an open mind and being able to recognize great ideas even when you aren't looking for them.

- New ideas almost always come about in one of two ways: when someone thinks up a new idea and when mistakes happen.

- If you stick slavishly to what you planned to do, you could miss better opportunities that might pop up along the way.

- If something comes up that you didn't intend, don't be so quick to discount it as being wrong.

- The most highly realized creative thinkers are open to the gifts of accidental brilliance.

CHAPTER 15

Stop Making Sense

New ideas don't make sense. In the contemporary order of things, that is.

> *History is littered with missed opportunities, when individuals or groups had wonderful new ideas that had all the potential to create tremendous improvement but never saw the light of day because the ideas didn't "make sense."*

How do I know this? Well, my answer won't make sense to you, so I won't try to explain. But I will point out some near misses that, if not for the efforts of a few determined souls, may not have gotten off the ground. Hey, "getting off the ground" is a good place to start!

AIRPLANE DELAYS

We all know what the Wright brothers did at Kitty Hawk. It amazes me to this day that a big bucket of bolts can fly. Well, they did it. The Wright brothers put it all together. Yes, they did it with the help of da Vinci and dozens of other pioneers in the physical sciences (see Chapter 10, "Collaborate with Genius").

Did the world beat a path to their cockpit door? Sorry.

"You mean there weren't hundreds of visionary captains of industry who saw the amazing potential of human flight?" you ask.

Well, no.

"Come on," you insist. "There had to have been at least a few open-minded American businesspeople who saw the potential for moving goods and passengers through the air from city to city, continent to continent, theme park to theme park."

Nope. Not a one.

The Wright brothers, having found no buyers for their high-flying idea stateside, had to go all the way to France to find a buyer for their irrational new concept. It just didn't make sense to the people of their time. "Flying like a bird?" This concept was too outrageous to penetrate the inertia of conventional thought that occupied the minds of all those who were approached with the opportunity to buy into this revolutionary idea early on.

Idea? Heck, the airplane wasn't just an idea. It was an industry. A way of life. A precedent-setting world shrinker.

But it just didn't make sense.

So, I guess you don't have to feel so bad when your boss or coworkers don't always see the wisdom of your new ideas. Don't worry—it just might be a sign of how radical your idea truly is. (Hey, you wouldn't be planning any trips to France in the near future, would you?)

LAST STITCH EFFORT

The airplane has to be an isolated case, right? Maybe too big for most people to get their minds around.

Hardly isolated.

Take the sewing machine. In fact, you might as well take this time-saving device across the Atlantic where the Wright brothers went to fly their new idea. Yup, that's what Elias Howe had to do to get someone to buy his newly patented device in 1846.

After a lifelong pursuit of perfecting the automatic stitching machine, this tailor-turned-inventor gave up on selling the patent to American business after having innumerable doors closed in his face. He took his idea eastward. He stopped in England where he found a buyer not only eager to take his new product to market, the scoundrel actually stole the patent and sent Howe back to the States empty-handed. Ouch.

THE POLITICS OF NEW IDEAS

The first of Thomas Edison's 1,093 patents was for an automatic vote counter he developed to make counting election ballots quicker, easier, and less prone to human error.

Well, the idea didn't make much sense to all the municipalities Edison showed it to (we dare not ask why they wouldn't want a more fool-proof method of tallying votes), so the yet-to-be most prolific inventor in U.S. history moved on and swore never to develop another product for the public sector. A promise he kept until the day he died.

I bring up these examples partly to encourage those of you who have perhaps encountered a bit of resistance to your new ideas to hang in there. Or, as Edison did, find a place to create where you might meet less resistance.

BUSINESS AS UNUSUAL

Of course, the reluctance of people to embrace new ideas is not reserved for great inventors. Hardly. Within my own client base I have heard many stories in which new ideas were accepted with far from open arms.

I heard a story told by an individual at the *Wall Street Journal* who played a major role in giving birth to one of the most revolutionary improvements to this fine publication in the past 50 years. He said it took him five years to get his comrades to see the wisdom of this concept. A concept that has gone on to add a whole new dimension to the periodical, not to mention millions of dollars in incremental income. I'm talking about the preprinted industry-focused inserts that the *Wall Street Journal* includes periodically in its editorial calendar.

"But, we're a newspaper," I can hear some of the dyed-in-the-worsted-wool-suit management types. "We print news, not . . . whatever this is." It just didn't make sense in the traditional scheme of things.

Capital One, another of my many fine clients and one of the largest, fastest-growing credit card companies in the world, was founded on an idea that didn't make sense—*balance transfer*, a concept that the entire credit card industry is based on today. When they were part of Signet Bank, some of the employees who went on to be pioneers at Capital

The Chairman mentioned your big idea at the big meeting. This is better than a raise. (Well, there's less of a tax implication anyway.)

Timeline of a great idea (continued)

Timeline of a lousy idea (continued)

One had to work nights and hire temporary help to handwrite checks to buy the credit balances from competing companies.

DON'T CHANGE THE CHANNEL

I heard Don Hewitt, founder of *60 Minutes*, the longest-running prime-time TV show of all time, say that people at CBS thought he was crazy with his far-out concept of an investigative news program in prime time.

I also heard the president of CBS say he thought Mark Burnett, the producer of *Survivor*, was crazy when he first broached that show's concept to the network.

Then there's the famous NBC internal memo telling the producers of the *Seinfeld* pilot that the concept would never fly. A show about nothing? Doesn't make sense. A stand-up comic doing stand-up in a sitcom. How could Hollywood possibly get its mind around such a radical idea?

HE DOTH PROTEST TOO MUCH

Even in a world where creativity is supposedly revered, it's fairly well known that Berry Gordy, head of Motown, had a hard time embracing Marvin Gaye's landmark *What's Goin' On?* album in 1971.

I can hear the less than harmonious voice of management crying, "But protest songs are for folkies from Greenwich Village."

Gaye's masterpiece, featuring songs such as "Mercy Mercy Me (the Ecology)," "Save the Children," and "Inner City Blues," went on to sell millions and is considered one of the top records of its time, one of the top records ever to come out of Motown.

Of course, all of these examples of ideas that survived in spite of much protest and lack of appreciation did indeed make it. Think of all the other brilliant ideas that did not make it because they didn't make sense.

> *It numbs my mind to think of all that has been lost because of lack of vision. Maybe it's a good thing that we'll never know what we're missing.*

Cheat Notes for Chapter 15:
Stop Making Sense

- *The rational mind defaults to what you know, what makes sense.*

- *New ideas don't "make sense" (the airplane, the sewing machine, rock 'n' roll, to name a few).*

- *Don't feel bad when your boss or coworkers don't always see the wisdom of your new ideas; it just might be a sign of how original your idea truly is.*

- *If your ideas meet with too much resistance too frequently, consider finding a place to create where you might meet less resistance.*

Redefining the Acceptable Range

Every individual and every corporate culture, it seems, has an acceptable range of thinking, a spectrum of consideration, a comfort zone in which they evaluate ideas.

> *The more open-minded people and more progressive companies obviously have broader acceptable ranges than their less open counterparts.*

This concept of "acceptable range" became apparent to me over the years when I first recognized a rather vague pattern of behavior following many of the brainstorming sessions I conducted. I also noticed that this acceptable range expanded as a result of the changed state people found themselves in after participating in one of my skills development programs, whether it was a two-hour Do-It-Yourself Lobotomy or a three-day Creative Camp.

Let me explain by recounting a conversation that happened on the way to the airport with a client. This discussion, following a brainstorming session, served as an epiphany for me in finally crystallizing the concept of acceptable range and how it limits creativity. My company was brought in to help a work group in a large corporation reduce the time-to-market cycle from 120 to 90 days to remain competitive in a particular business category. I'll change the names and the business category to protect the confidentiality of the company involved.

MOMENT OF ACCEPTABLE TRUTH

"So, are you happy with the final output?" I asked the client, knowing I was likely to get an affirmative answer because we had just completed a session that reduced their time-to-market cycle from 120 days to 87 days, actually three days shorter than the target.

"I'm very happy," said the client, smiling at me.

I probed further. We had uncovered hundreds of ways to shorten their production cycle, dozens of timesaving steps, it seemed, at each stage of the production process. "So, what are some of the newer, more radical ideas that wound up in the final mix?" I asked.

The client wrinkled his brow as he pondered this question. He finally spoke up. "I don't think there were any new ideas in the final mix," he said, not the least bit smugly.

I pretended to remain cool. These people had just paid my company a good deal of money to help them through the birth canal of this process. They had been a great client over the years, bringing us in frequently to help them tackle big challenges and opportunities. I hoped the answer to my question was not going to backfire on me. I had to get to the bottom of this.

"Alan," I said. "You're happy with the session?"

"That's right," he answered.

"And we *did* come up with a ton of new ideas, didn't we?" I queried.

"That's right," he affirmed.

"But the final output included nothing you hadn't seen before."

"Yes, that's true," he said.

"I'm sorry," I admitted, "but I don't get it."

He thought for a while before he proceeded. "Well, we may have had all of those ideas before, in different forms and at different times, when tossing around ways to get to market quicker, but we never pulled the trigger on them prior to today."

I remained silent, taking in this interesting phenomenon. My client continued with his explanation, "I guess stirring up the pot with so many new ideas, many of which were pretty radical, kind of put some of our old radical ideas into perspective and made them look a little more practical, a little safer."

"Interesting," I said. Then I fell into a brief silence to think about what had just become clear to me.

We had solved my client's problem. He and his team had uncovered a plethora of truly new ideas, but they were going with a solution that included none of them. And they were happy.

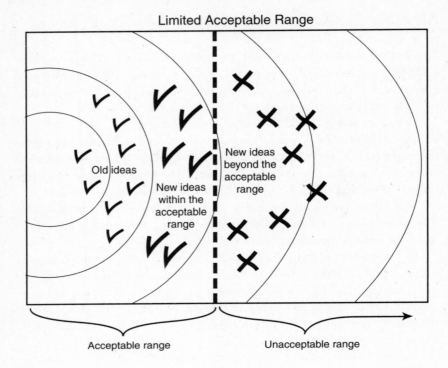

Then and there it occurred to me that I had seen this circumstance before, a company or individual who didn't pull the trigger on new ideas but was nonetheless happy with the brainstorming session conducted to find new ideas. I had been part of this strange phenomenon before, but now I more fully understood it. They had *expanded* their acceptable range of ideas. They had done it by coming up with an abundance of new ideas, many of which were beyond the previous fringe of acceptability, and, by contrast, the old fringe ideas now seemed less scary and risky. In very much the same way as Lewis and Clark's exploration of the great Northwest made the previous frontier boundary seem less remote and more welcoming. A lot of things fell into place for me that day.

TURNING UP THE SOIL

With most brainstorming sessions I've been involved in, we are looking for a great many ideas, whether it's new products or services, promotional ideas, customer support, or whatever.

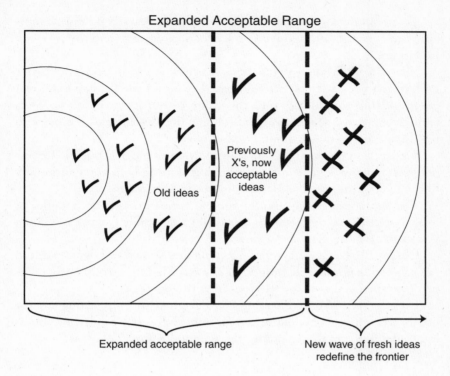

In some sessions, however, we are looking for only one ultimate idea—for instance, when brainstorming a name for a product, a company, or a URL.

I'd say that in about half of the naming sessions that I have led, the final name is discovered after the brainstorming proper. The first few times this happened, frankly, I was somewhat concerned that my brainstorming process was somehow flawed or that I didn't push hard enough or far enough. But then I realized, again with the help of a client conversation or two, that without the brainstorming session, the name that emerged days or weeks later might not have been uncovered. "It grew from the soil we turned up together," commented one client. Yes, *that,* and perhaps an expanded acceptable range.

IS YOUR ACCEPTABLE RANGE MORE ACCEPTING?

A big part of being fully realized, creatively, is recognizing the value of fresh ideas when you see them.

This book has systematically been helping you open your acceptable range of thought to give you a broader playing field upon which to operate.

The early chapters of the book were written to help you better understand creativity, as we addressed many of the fundamental elements of this wonderful stuff: the value of not knowing so you can wonder more, the role of problem solving, the character of change, and the distinction between creativity and talent.

The section on creative thinking tools—the Do-It-Yourself Lobotomy instruments—gave you the thinking skills to help you continually find new ideas that will expand your acceptable range.

The discourse on accidental genius demonstrated the benefits of open-mindedness, the need for a broader acceptable range even when you're not looking for a new idea.

Chapter 16 has asked you to "stop making sense" and demonstrated how a narrow acceptable range can be expanded. It so frequently takes perseverance and courage to proceed with new ideas.

Chapter 18, "Mind Farming," is designed to help managers (or others who consciously manage their own skill sets) to cultivate thinking traits that lead to expanding the acceptable range of ideas.

Don't Break the Rules, Break the Ruler

Creativity is about originating ideas. Much of what this book covers is the active generation of these original concepts. After all, in today's pit-bull-eat-pit-bull competitive environment, just waiting for creative brilliance to strike is not enough; we need to make it happen when and where we need fresh ideas. Like genetically engineered food, our ideation process needs to be bulked up, and bulked up big, to stay in the game. That said, if you can open your acceptable range of thought and keep it open, that is like keeping your creative soil in a constant state of proper nutritional health so that the bounty of fresh ideas simply grows, blossoms, and reseeds itself for further growth and regeneration, on and on, indefinitely.

That is how the great creative minds work. By constantly exploring new territory. By constantly developing fresh ideas.

As they attack challenges and opportunities, a lot of people say, "Let's break the rules!" But even when they *do* create new ideas, I too often see people ignore those new concepts that may take their efforts forward in favor of playing it safe with tried-and-true solutions. They may have broken the rules in coming up with ideas, but they have not broken the ruler in measuring the acceptability of their new ideas.

If you break the rules *and* the ruler, through better understanding and by mastering the techniques in this book, you can bring yourself to an amazing place of discovery. You'll find an exciting new level where there is less to understand and learn, a state of mind that doesn't try to be creative, but simply *is* creative. At that point, everything and anything is within your acceptable range. At that point, you are a totally realized person in a creative sense.

Timeline of a great idea (continued)

Timeline of a lousy idea (continued)

"I'll never be so quick to commit
to that kind of idea again."

Cheat Notes for Chapter 16:
Redefining the Acceptable Range

- *Acceptable range of thinking: when evaluating ideas, the spectrum of consideration that feels comfortable.*

- *Expanding your acceptable range of thought gives you a broader playing field.*

- *To expand your acceptable range, don't just break the rules, break the ruler.*

- *By contrast, new ideas beyond the previous fringe of acceptability make old fringe ideas seem less scary and less risky.*

- *Continue expanding your acceptable range to achieve a state of mind that doesn't try to be creative, but simply is creative — then anything is within your acceptable range.*

Selling Creative Ideas Requires Its Own Creativity

It's one thing to come up with a great idea. *Conceiving,* so to speak. It's quite another thing to give birth to it and raise it to maturity. And the trickiest part of that postconception routine is getting others to embrace the new idea, what we commonly refer to as *selling* it.

When I address groups on the topic of creativity, I often ask, "How many of you sell?" Unless I'm working with a sales force, I almost always encounter only a smattering of hands. Most people don't consider themselves salespeople. They don't take selling seriously, they don't approach it consciously, and they wonder why so many of their ideas don't see fruition because other people won't buy them.

AN EPIDEMIC OF UNREALIZED CREATIVE IDEAS

As consultants, my fellow creative thinking coaches and I work in all kinds of companies, in a wide variety of industries, under all kinds of conditions.

> *One thing that's common to all companies is that the quality of the ideas that come out of the other end of the machine, on average, is never as good as the quality of the ideas the people actually conceive.*

We often call this the *creative sell success rate.* In many ways, it is to people in business what batting average is to baseball players, what box office receipts are to the movie industry.

I believe that an idea is not great if it doesn't ultimately see the light of day. That, to me, is like hitting a home run in batting practice. It doesn't count for anything. The real superstars in baseball are the players who do it in prime time, just as the real winners in any other industry are the people who have new ideas that actually become reality.

The One Club for Copy and Art, one of the largest (if not the largest) organizations of advertising creatives in the world, has an event called "The night of the living dead." At this event they honor great ads that never ran. With all due respect to the One Club, which as a former board member I'm very supportive of, I'm sorry, but if an ad never ran, it simply can't be a great ad. To glorify these failures to sell "great" ideas is to encourage laziness (or at least not to encourage the selling of great ideas). The proof? The so-called winners of these awards are not the real shakers and movers in the ad business.

You have to perform in the real world, my friends, if you want to succeed at anything. All unqualified, uncompromised success? Well, no, not totally. I may be an idealist, but I'm not a raving idealist. I will admit that there are inevitably some concessions in the process of bringing almost any idea to maturity. And I suppose I should never expect any company to have absolutely all of its ideas slip totally unscathed through the obstacle course of reality. But I can tell you from my extensive experience in this area that the most highly realized individuals and organizations, from a creativity standpoint, don't do it solely with brute creative strength, forcing their ideas upon others; they also know how to sell their ideas. To use a phrase I much prefer, "They know how to get others to embrace their ideas."

Staying on the topic of advertising for a moment, a number of years ago I did an informal analysis of what accounts for exemplary creative achievement in advertising. I did a general but fairly far-reaching ad-industry-wide Creative ForceField Analysis (see page 251). What I discovered is that the agencies and companies doing the most creative work don't necessarily have a corner on the best creative people, copywriters, and art directors. As it was, their people mostly came and went, but didn't always perform as well elsewhere. However, those companies *did* overachieve in the area of *selling* their best work. To put an exclamation mark on that point, the then-reigning ad agency of the year, Goodby, Silverstein & Partners, hired away two people from my ad agency, an agency that many people considered "creatively driven." But they weren't creative people per se who were cherry-picked from my staff—they were account people who could sell great work.

THE PROOF IS IN THE SELLING

Is your company achieving its potential creatively? The proof is in the selling.

If the final product is compromised in any way, ask yourself, "Were the concessions absolutely necessary, or did someone simply not do a good job shepherding the idea through to completion?" In other words, "Did we simply not sell the idea?"

If your ideas are compromised too deeply too often, maybe it's not the quality of the ideas or the execution; maybe it's a lack of ability to have others see the brilliance in the idea or the lack of ability to get others to let go of their preconceptions long enough to see the potential of the new idea. (Do I dare say the inability for others to lobotomize themselves, conceptually? Or perhaps your inability to lobotomize them? Ouch.)

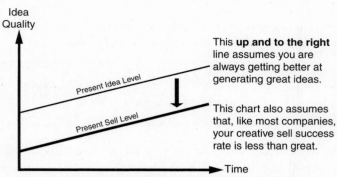

The creative sell success rate at most companies looks like this.

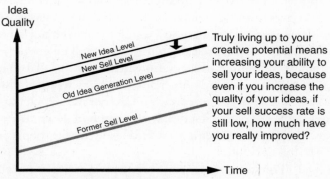

A higher sell rate narrows the gap.

Now you might be asking what all this talk of selling ideas has to do with creativeness. Well, actually, it has a great deal to do with creativeness. As we illustrated early on in this book, creativity is problem solving. Ask anyone who is in sales for a living and they'll tell you that selling is problem solving as well. So you shouldn't have to get an Einsteinian haircut to deduce that selling requires creativity.

In my role as a creative thinking coach I am often brought in to work with sales forces. I must tell you, the best of their ranks are as brilliant creatively as are any people I encounter in the business world—and that includes the self-proclaimed ground zero of creativity, ad agency creative departments. The best salespeople have curious minds, they have active minds, they seek fresh perspectives. This sounds a lot like the "dreamer" personality type from Chapter 18, "Mind Farming." Read on, read on.

ANOTHER LEVEL OF CREATIVITY

To anyone reading this book who has ever wished more of their ideas would be embraced by those around them, I challenge you:

> *Use these concepts, wisdom, and practices not just to come up with great ideas, but also to* sell *them.*

Asking better questions is a great place to start. Even before you start thinking of the problem, think about the people you need to sell the solution to. And don't guess what's on their mind—ask them.

As for applying 100 MPH Thinking to selling, when you've worked very hard to conceive and develop an idea, you don't consider only one way to get it across to others, do you? Using the law of large numbers, if you think of just two ways to sell your ideas, you'll be giving yourself twice the chance of finding a successful way to sell. A full 100 percent increase, all for thinking of only one additional way to sell. How about three ideas for a 200 percent increase? Or five ideas? Or 25 ideas? With many sales strategies or tactics, it may not boil down to an either-or situation. If selling the idea one way doesn't work, then you have other plans to fall back on.

As for 180° Thinking, well, you've heard of reverse psychology, haven't you? My wife and I have been selling antiques for years. We learned decades ago that if you *don't* want to sell it, everyone wants to buy it. We used to hide certain not-for-sale items behind a door in our house, only to find that more than one antiques dealer who called on us would discover it there and try to talk us out of it. After a while, when we really wanted to sell something we'd just "hide it" behind that magic door.

21 Tips for Selling Creative Ideas

All the tools covered in this book can play a role in helping you sell your ideas. Of course, there is a great deal more to selling than just the Do-It-Yourself Lobotomy tools in this book. And although I don't profess to be an expert on selling in the strict sense of the word, I do have some valuable tips to pass along that just might help you raise your *creative sell success rate.*

Are They Really Your Best Ideas?
The first tip for selling your best ideas is to make sure they *are* your best ideas. I see so many people wasting their energy—exerting their brilliant sales effort or even their lousy sales effort—trying to sell bad ideas. That's like building an elaborate restaurant business around a lousy chef.

So the first tip to help you sell better ideas is to actually *have* better ideas. Sounds pretty basic, doesn't it? Well, I can tell you that I've had a good many corporate clients, including ad agencies, ask me to help them with their sales hit rate when in reality the first thing they need to do is improve the product they're selling.

When It's Time to Sell, It's Too Late to Sell
Many years ago I facilitated an international forum of top managers in one of the major service industries. We covered a plethora of topics: attracting and motivating the best people, defining and articulating corporate vision, and so forth, all kinds of issues that top managers typically focus their energies on. We also covered selling, which of course is the lifeblood of any business. When the dust settled on three days of exploration, the major concept that kept resonating within this group was summed up in these few words, "When it's time to sell, it's too late to sell."

To a person, we all agreed that the biggest part of selling was the relationship the company had with its clients. If they had a great relationship prior to the sale, even a shaky, less-than-perfect sales presentation usually resulted in a fair degree of success. But if the relationship was rocky . . . if the relationship was grounded in anything less than great trust and respect, the sale was invariably a bloody, unsuccessful venture.

With that brilliant deduction said, there are still some things you can do beyond relationship building to help others embrace your new ideas. Some of them follow.

The Tao of Selling

A major mistake many people make when trying to get others to embrace their ideas is doing just that—*trying* to get others to embrace their ideas, and trying too hard. This is one place where most people use 180° Thinking almost without thinking. And it's not always a good thing.

Here's how it usually works: Someone shows resistance to a new idea, and what does the parent of that idea usually do? What any proud parents do when their offspring is criticized. They resist.

> *The* Tao Te Ching, *that book of ancient Eastern wisdom, teaches that resistance meets resistance and surrender meets surrender.*

Yes, it's natural to push back. But if that's not usually going to help your cause, why are you doing it? Sure, sometimes we have to stand firm for our ideas, but if you make that your first defense, it may be your last.

A number of times when I was a creative director, I helped young advertising people get this point, often while they watched in open-mouthed disbelief. When clients expressed resistance to an idea, I would often say, "That's interesting. Would you explain that to me?" I didn't defend the idea. I didn't remain neutral. I just softened to their point of view and gave them some credence. At that point, clients knew I was listening to them, and guess what happened most often? They listened to me. Oh, I didn't sell the ad every time, but I had a very high batting average. And, importantly, I didn't make a mortal enemy of someone who had a great deal of influence on the outcome of my agency's ideas.

Have Clear, Written Objectives

When working on a project that requires creative thinking (are there any that don't?), before you even start the work, set clear objectives between yourself and those you need to sell the idea to, whether they be people inside your company, outside your company, or both. And not only should you set clear objectives, you should write them down, because then it's not a matter of "I like it," "you like it," or "you don't like it," it's a matter of "does this satisfy the objective?"

Yes, there's still some room for interpretation there, but clearly defined objectives remove most of the wiggle room that so often causes misinterpretation and disagreement.

Believe me, this is very valuable, the writing-down part. If the objectives are in ink before work starts, then both parties can't suddenly have dramatically different recollections of earlier events.

Have Clear Roles. Written

Another thing to do is have clear roles in advance. It's pretty simple. Before you start the project, know who's going to play the role of coming up with the idea and who's going to play the role of reacting to it, providing guidance or buying the idea.

This may seem obvious if you're the ideator—it's my job to come up with the idea, it's your job to sell it—but if you have it clearly articulated in advance, in writing, then in the heat of a discussion that does not become an issue. If roles are not articulated clearly in advance and you present your idea to someone who starts tinkering, things can get kind of fuzzy and messy. You might say, "Hey, wait a minute, it's *my* job to come up with the idea. It's just your job to react to it, and if you don't like it then I'll go back and work on it." That's the wrong time to define roles, because then it appears that you're defending your *idea,* as opposed to defending your role in the creative process.

Many organizations have different roles for what may appear to be the same players. Even within the same industry and for identical titles this is true. I see different companies in a given industry where people with the same titles perform very different functions. So don't oversimplify this. Discuss it openly and write down the roles clearly. This isn't just a title thing, it's a who's-going-to-do-what thing, a professional-boundaries thing. And we all know that good fences make good neighbors.

The most abused title in the advertising business is that of creative director. The creative director should be the person who has ultimate say on things creative, but in many companies that person is not the creative director—it's the person the creative director answers to (the president, the owner, whomever). Whereas the creative director may have the title, the other individual has the authority. Even if I don't agree with the charade, at least roles do not become an issue when selling ideas.

Blowing Your Own Sale

Another tip on getting people to embrace your ideas is to avoid certain terms that can only lead to disaster:

"This is my favorite idea."
"I think this idea is great."
"This idea is just like . . ."

These and other such terms usually mean trouble. People you're selling ideas to really don't care what your favorite idea is; they want the *best* idea. They really don't care whether you think it's great. Oh, they may ask you, but in the end they want the best idea, the most effective idea, the idea that will produce the greatest results.

Similarly, "just like" doesn't do much in a unique marketing situation that needs a fresh solution. In fact, by definition, it can't be very creative if it's "just like" something. Even saying it's "somewhat like," which you can use for a support point perhaps later, is a bad idea to lead off with.

Yes, some people you're selling to may need the comfort of knowing that someone's been there before, but in many cases "just like" are code words for disaster.

Basically, the best way to sell an idea is not to talk about what's *your* favorite or what *you* like, but to talk about the objective and how your idea will help reach the objective. In this regard, advertising creative people are often their own worst enemies. A few years ago I wrote a piece in *Communication Arts* entitled, "You too can speak like a Harvard MBA." In this tongue-in-cheek article, I gave advertising creative people sound bites to use in front of clients to help them appear to have a clue about business: "This will move the needle" and other such arcane expressions. Creativity in business is not a beauty contest. This is commerce. What you like means nothing if it doesn't make the cash register ring.

Don't Have All the Answers

Here's a tip on selling that I learned early in my career. When I was about to start my ad agency over 20 years ago, I read an article about what the best clients look for in ad agencies. In this very helpful article, one individual said something to this effect:

> *"I don't want someone who has all the answers; I want someone who will get all the answers."*

If you have all the answers, which is the tendency when you sell (you try to have all your ducks in a row, you try to answer all the concerns), you could be hurting your cause more than helping. Even if you literally have all the answers, and even if your answers are correct, people don't always value them when they're just thrown around so readily.

Nobody's that smart. Nobody has all the answers. If you're stumped, or even just unsure and don't have the answer, don't guess. Don't B.S. people. Say instead, "I don't know. I'll get back to you on that." I can tell you from experience that many people find this honesty very refreshing.

Frankly, I use this technique sometimes even when I *do* have the answers. Why? Because if I have a ready answer and they have a ready objection, they're probably still stuck in their objection place. If I say, "Let me get back to you on that," they may cool off on their objection. If I come back with the answer when they're in a cooler place, maybe I'll have more success.

Another thing about this approach: Not only will they believe you're more thoughtful about it, but, frankly, *you may actually develop a better answer* in that extra time you allot yourself.

And one last selling secret in this area: You can charge people more if you take more time. (Only kidding. . . . Well, half kidding.)

Prepare for Success

Perhaps the greatest college basketball coach of all time, John Wooden, who led the UCLA dynasty during the 1960s and 1970s, said, "Failure to prepare is to prepare to fail." I see so many people go off half-cocked, ready to sell their ideas without the necessary preparation. Being prepared means thinking through how you're going to sell your idea, thinking through how others are going to perceive it, thinking about objections that might arise—again, not necessarily to have all the answers but simply to be prepared. It's utterly amazing how few people really prepare to sell their ideas. Then they wonder why their success rate is so low.

Another part of preparation is rehearsing. The best salespeople rehearse. Most people I encounter in business rehearse their sales pitch very little. The best salespeople rehearse a great deal. Ever wonder how they got to be the best?

Know Your Audience

Whom are you selling your idea to? Whom are you talking to? Your presentation, your preparation, might be very different if you're selling to *this* person versus *that* person.

Know the individuals, know their priorities, know what turns them on, and know what scares them. In the advertising business, I worked with a good many very smart people. Most were middle managers, and most had a certain level of fear of their top management. You need to recognize that. I have heard people in the ad business say, "If the idea doesn't make their palms sweat then it isn't a good idea." I say, if it makes their palms sweat, they're less likely to be allies in helping you sell this idea, and they're more likely to be obstacles.

I'm not saying you can't present an idea that might make them a little nervous. I'm just saying that you need to know them, know what makes their palms sweat, do your homework, and do your best to avoid the terms and context that might lead to sweaty palms. Sometimes it means answering the objections before you show them the idea. That doesn't mean saying, "Here's an objection you might have, and here's how I'm going to answer it." It simply means providing the information, the context, and the examples before you show them the idea. That can be quite easily done.

Know What and Who Is Behind Your Audience

If you know your audience, you'll know the important issues and the sensitive places and how to deal with them. If you don't know your audience, you won't know these things and how to deal with them. You are, essentially, operating in a minefield.

I like to know my audience's audience extremely well. Again, if middle managers are fearful of upper management, then I want to know the upper management, too. If I can't get to know upper management personally, I want to know them through speeches, through articles they've written, through the annual report. In fact one of the best selling tools I've used (it may sound like manipulation, but I mean it absolutely sincerely) is the phrase, "In your annual report your chairman says . . ." Of course, the annual report! This is the direction the company is headed. I'm helping the individuals I'm working with to align themselves with the direction of the company. Wow! When I point out that my idea is based on what their chairman says, it comforts them, takes some of the risk out of a new idea, and in many cases helps them to like it before they've even seen it.

"Two Rabbis Walk into a Massage Parlor . . ."

Have fun when you sell. You know, there's a good reason that old-time salesmen used to walk in and open with a joke, like a regular Shecky

Loman. People love a good yuk. Sometimes what you're selling has serious consequences. So lighten it up. Have some fun.

I'm not necessarily saying walk in with your rabbi joke, but I prefer a light atmosphere come show time. Sometimes that's really hard to do because so much is at stake. But sometimes the more that's at stake, the more nervous energy there is, and then they'll laugh at anything. Have some fun. Talk about something light. Talk about positive things before you get into the heavy stuff. It's like the dancing that Muhammad Ali does before he delivers the knockout punch. I don't want to put this in the context of combat, but it's just a matter of keeping it light before you get into the heavy stuff.

Up Your Curtain

Another method that helps to sell ideas is theater. I like to use the presentation as an opportunity to get people excited, to entertain them. People love to be entertained. People will pay $80 for a theater ticket, $8 to see a movie, $75 for a concert seat, $60 for a ball game. You can give them entertainment for free when you're selling, and it just might grease the skids to help your idea see the light of day. I'm not talking about song and dance in the cheap carnival sense—although sometimes it could border on that if that works.

I got a big lesson in using theater to sell when many years ago the ad agency I was working for lost a new business pitch to a guy who ran a very small creative shop. To neutralize the size advantage and make a couple of other points as well, this daring small agency owner carried a half-dozen mannequins into the prospect's conference room to help make his pitch. Word was the client felt the empty suits made about as much of a contribution to the meeting as the other agency's phalanx of executives, and at a much lower hourly rate.

⚜

SALESMANSHIP LONG ON THEATRICS

Theater can take lots of forms. One of my favorite theater tricks is something I performed years ago. This particular act was more pantomime than song and dance. We said nothing. In fact, a passive, static prop provided all the theater. This particular selling idea came directly out of the advertising idea that we were trying to sell, which came directly out of this product's primary point of difference. My ad agency worked for Lotus Development Corporation, and we were presenting an idea for what they called a "document processor."

Lotus was late to get into word processing, so the company tried to leapfrog word processing with a concept for a "document processor," designed for lengthy, complex technical documents. At that time, the top-selling word processors, Microsoft Word and WordPerfect, were built primarily for business letters. With our niche being long documents, we had an idea for a print ad that was long. In fact, it was a double-gate, 16-page advertisement to run in *Time* magazine, nearly 70 inches long. To my knowledge it was the longest ad ever in *Time*, the longest from the standpoint of length when it was folded out, and probably the most expensive single, one-time insertion at the time in that magazine—about a million dollars, I believe.

To sell the concept of long document processing, and to sell the concept of a long ad, we created a tangible selling device. Our *theater* was a runner on the floor that looked like a massive, oversized long document. When people got out of the elevator, our runner led them 100 yards to the conference room down the hall. They were forced to actually walk on this very long document. What we did was to take five pages, have them blown up and silk-screened onto some 15-foot-long canvas pieces, and then we repeated it and stitched it all together. It was a production nightmare, but it was theater. It was event marketing designed to sell an idea. And I must tell you that the clients walked into the room already liking an ad they hadn't even seen yet.

❖

Can I Show You Our Suit, Sir?

Give people choice. When you're selling an idea, give people some selection. Don't just show them one idea. Nobody ever walked into a haberdashery that had only one suit. Nobody ever walked into an automobile showroom that had only one car. Nobody ever walked into a computer showroom that had only one computer. People want choice. Give it to them.

When I first started in the ad business, a senior writer told me that if you show people one idea, one of two things will happen. If they like you, they'll say they like it. If they don't like you, they'll say they don't like it. But if you show them three ideas and ask them which is best, they'll probably tell you the truth, and if they don't like you and tell you they like A, you'll know it's B or C that's best.

Of course, to give people choice forces you to have more than one idea. And, I'm not saying have one good idea and five bad ones; they all have to be good. But, heck, if you're using 100 MPH Thinking, you've got more ideas than you know what to present anyway. Offer them a choice. Many people are afraid of taking that leap. Because a lot of people don't believe they can have lots of good ideas. Well, I believe you can, and I've been around enough high-quality creative people who believe they can—and do. Besides that, an interesting thing happens when you present choice. A 180° experience, so to speak.

You see, most people in trying to sell an idea are really just trying to get someone else to buy the single idea they want them to take. Well, going back to the Tao of selling (i.e., force meets force and surrender meets surrender), when you try to force people, they forcibly say no, quite typically. When you offer them a choice, quite frequently after absorbing the many choices, the sellee will ask, "Well, what do you recommend?" And then you can make your recommendation. Easy.

You may go in with a favorite, but I will tell you that if you have an open mind, and this has happened to me on many occasions, after judging the reaction of your audience to your numerous ideas, your favorite might change. If you go in with a hard-and-fast recommendation, then change your stance when you hear a reaction, you could look like a fool or you could look like you're open-minded, depending on how you play it. But when you offer a choice, quite often people will ask what you recommend. And as a professional, isn't that what you want?

The great irony is that if you recommend only one idea, they look for a choice. I work with ad agencies that say, "We present only one concept per ad." And I'll ask how often they present only one. "Well, we present one five times in a row until we get it right." Well, then you're not presenting just one. You're having a very, very lengthy choice session (and very expensive, I might add). And how often do they come back and take choice number 2 after seeing numbers 3 and 4? It does happen, and it's a waste of time, effort, and money.

I like offering choice early on in the creative process. I don't like offering a choice of finished ideas. That's a lot of wasted effort. I like offering people a choice of ideas that are in earlier stages of development. But make sure they're all at similar stages of development,

Timeline of a great idea (continued)

Timeline of a lousy idea (continued)

"I should have gone to Tom Monahan's Creative Camp."

because sometimes the ones further along in development have an unfair advantage.

Conviction Leads to Execution

If you want to take an idea from the conceptual stage to execution, nothing works like conviction. I'm not talking about force alone. I'm talking about a genuine belief that the idea you have is going to succeed in a very big way. When you use 100 MPH Thinking (often in concert with other of the Do-It-Yourself Lobotomy tools), you inevitably have many ideas from which to cull your shortlist. It makes presenting many ideas much easier, but more important than that, it gives you conviction.

There is a difference between feigned conviction, which I see all the time in business, and the real deal, or deal maker, as it were. When you present one idea, or even two or three ideas, to those who must buy in to bring them to fruition, they may react to your final recommendation by asking, "Is this the best idea?" It's a pretty fair bet that you'll have to say, "Yes this is the best idea," even though you can't look them straight in the eye when you say it, because you've looked at only a handful of ideas—you really don't know whether it's the best idea. There is absolutely no way you can answer with authentic conviction.

However, if you look at 100 potential solutions to their problem, present several, and make a final recommendation, then, when asked the same question, you can look them straight in the eye and answer, "Absolutely!" with firm conviction.

The fact of the matter is that you really don't *know* if the new idea is best. (I mentioned earlier that you never come up with your best idea.) And, with a new idea, there's never proof that it *will* work. (Of course, there's no guarantee an old idea will work, either.) But in the heat of an important sales pitch, it's important that *you* think it's your best idea, that you have unfailing and absolute conviction in your idea. And genuine conviction makes the sale almost every time.

Bring People in Early

A couple more things about selling: When you show people ideas that are undergoing development, they can take ownership. They can say, "Hey, I kind of like where that's going." Then, after you fully develop "their" idea, they are already onboard. I must tell you that people don't generally derail projects they have a vested interest in. Show them ideas early so they can be partners in the solution.

Again, in the advertising business I've seen many creatives who are petrified of showing others their ideas as they materialize, even internally. They often hold back from sharing ideas with the suits until they're running out the door. Then all kinds of bad stuff can happen . . . the suits aren't prepared to sell . . . they don't know what's on your mind . . . they don't know what your recommendation is . . . they have seconds to make up their mind instead of being part of the process . . . and quite often they will decide what they're going to sell regardless of what *you* want them to present. Not good.

When you involve people early, you take a leap, but again, having crystal clear roles defines who creates and who reacts. Even if their reaction doesn't support your point of view, it's good to know this early. As an advertising creative person, I used the early in-house presentation as a gauge of what the client was going to think. I don't want to be ambushed by the client's objections at the moment of truth; I want to know in advance what the objections may or may not be. That's why I like having this interim, internal meeting.

"They Killed the Idea." (Oh, Really?)

This is an aspect of selling that a lot of people miss. We are most frequently selling ideas. How we dress them up is not the idea, it's the execution. If the way you dress up the idea determines whether the idea lives or dies, then it's not an idea you're selling; it's an execution of an idea, or a very shallow idea, at best. So, for instance, when I hear advertising creative people say, "They killed the headline, so they killed the ad," I answer, "No, they killed the headline. The idea of the ad may very well still be alive. Write another headline."

Often, there are lots of headlines that can articulate a concept. Likewise, in any field there are lots of ways to execute an idea. If there are *not* lots of headlines that can articulate your concept, then it's likely a very shallow concept. That's what's wrong with pun headlines; that's what's wrong with pun visuals. If they kill the pun, they've killed the idea, because it's often a very shallow idea.

I believe that for the most part people remember ideas, not execution. They remember the primary concept behind things, not so much the manifestation of the idea itself. When people tell you about a movie, they very rarely recount the dialogue or the art direction or the stage direction. They relate the idea of the movie. People rarely come away with details, even though details play an important role in articulating the story, mood, or message. It's the same way with ads and many other products and services. They'll tell you the concept of the ad; there are lots of different words that can play off the concept. (There are exceptions. Budweiser's "Wassup?" is a good example because the execution and the idea were very tightly integrated. In most ads that is not the case.)

Lose the Battles to Win the War

> *I see people holding onto the little things that really don't matter in the end.*

In so doing they often wind up losing the war, as in not making the sale. I see advertising copywriters die on their swords for body copy. I like great ad text as well as the next person, but look at the readership scores. Nobody reads body copy. Okay, correction: Maybe 15 percent of people read a well-read ad, but only 2 percent of people read body copy on the average ad. Don't die on your sword. Don't draw your line in the sand over individual words or other execution details.

In other areas, when things get torn apart in the selling (or non-selling) process, ask yourself, "Is the basic concept going to stay intact?" Great, then let go of what didn't sell and go back and rework the details. I'm not saying you can't explain your details better and come back later and have some answers on details, but don't kill the whole idea because some of the details died.

When the Close Ruins the Deal

I so often hear about salespeople going in for the close, and I'm sorry, but I believe that is an old-fashioned concept that doesn't treat the sellee as an important player.

To me that's often manipulation and an unfair tactic, going in for the kill. I don't mind asking for the order under many conditions, but under just as many conditions I recommend *not* asking for the order, particularly relative to truly creative ideas. I recommend saying, "This is the new idea; now before you commit to a yea or a nay, why don't you think about it?" You can walk out of the room for 10 minutes; you can call back tomorrow. But you don't have to have the answer right now.

Putting people on the spot to answer definitively yes or no often forces them to state a conservative answer, the easy answer, which is often *no, maybe not,* or *I don't think so.* Because, particularly when you're showing new ideas, people are a little uncertain. We've talked about the fear of coming up with new ideas; well there's fear in *buying* new ideas, too. And often the early reaction is a fearful one. So don't put people on the spot. Don't force them to make a decision when they're in a fear place.

Expand the Acceptable Range, Even in Selling

In Chapter 16, "Redefining the Acceptable Range," I discuss how sometimes when ideating, the win is not necessarily in going with *the* new idea, but in merely expanding the "acceptable range." When you expand this range of acceptability, you can often act on previously unembraced ideas, ideas that were not acted on earlier because they were outside the comfort zone of some people. The same is true in selling.

Show many ideas, and show some ideas that you believe are outside of the acceptable range. Of course, you must make sure they're all on strategy, but if they're outside the acceptable range from a style standpoint or a tone standpoint, you're still playing fair. Don't put them so far over the edge that you lose credibility. However, a few permutations beyond the acceptable range is fine. This strategy often puts the other ideas, those that may otherwise have defined the risk fringe, somewhat within the acceptable range. Thus when you ask, "What do you think?" or when you give them time to reflect, they may now be willing to go with a new idea, even if it's not the far outer fringe.

Selling the Unknown

As I mentioned very early in this book, new ideas are part of the unknown—if they're truly original, that is. At this point in the book I shouldn't have to explain or defend the value of new ideas. This is not a book about the tried-and-true and the obvious. If you want lessons on selling the tried-and-true and the obvious, there are hundreds, probably thousands, of books that will help you. This book is about coming up with fresh ideas and using just as many creative resources to *sell* those new ideas.

The Secret to Selling Is Very Small

The secret to selling creative ideas is very small. It's what I call "the zone." It's that happy place where the seller and the sellee can peacefully coexist. Being creative is hard enough. Selling creative ideas can be even trickier if you're not equally resourceful in your approach. There are many frustrated creative people who have great ideas but can't get anyone to buy them. I might suggest

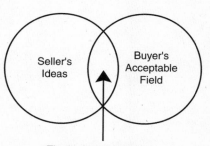

The Selling Zone

Seller's Ideas

Buyer's Acceptable Field

The happy place where people buy ideas.

it's less a case of closed-minded buyers than perhaps a case of closed-minded sellers. They don't understand that if an idea isn't in that happy place or can't expand the buyer's acceptable range, then it just isn't a great idea.

I close this chapter with a story about a young lady who once free-lanced for me at my ad agency. After busily working up a number of concepts to help solve a client's communications challenge, this bright-eyed, ponytailed young woman proudly brought some tissues into my office for some feedback. I put a handful of the better ideas aside, gave her some constructive feedback on them, and told her that they were very nice ideas. She beamed like a third-grader who'd just finished a test early. "But you realize," I said, "I can't present these to the client."

She knitted her brow instantly. I continued, "These ads are nice creatively, but they're not on strategy."

"You mean all those great creative ads that Leonard/Monahan wins awards for are also on strategy?" she said incredulously.

"Well, yeah," I said matter-of-factly.

She turned on her heel and went back to her office, I'm sure thinking about something quite similar to my earlier zone illustration.

Cheat Notes for Chapter 17: Selling Creative Ideas Requires Its Own Creativity

- On average, the quality of the ideas executed is never as good as the quality of the ideas actually conceived.

- It's not a great idea if it doesn't ultimately see the light of day.

- The real winners are the people who have new ideas that actually become reality.

- If your ideas are compromised too deeply too often, maybe it's not the quality of the ideas or the execution; maybe it's a lack of ability to have others see the brilliance in the idea.

- Identify the people you need to sell the idea to. And don't guess what's on their minds. Ask them.

CHAPTER 18

Mind Farming

How to Identify and Develop Creative Thinkers in Your Organization

This chapter has been written principally for people who manage others. If you're not a manager, you can learn a great deal about managing yourself for greater creative achievement. You may also learn more about what your manager might be looking for in you.

When running my ad agency years ago I found that there were many critical decisions that affected the quality and the success of our relationship with any given client and the creativity of the work we did for that client. Of all the decisions we made as managers that contributed to the success of an account team the most important by far was the choice of exactly who made up that team.

This talent selection process was particularly critical to me, as creative director, when assembling the copywriter and art director duo who would lead the creative development process on that account. Would they have the horses to do the job? Would they match up with the client's needs? Would they require a great deal of supervision or free me up for other fronts?

I often found myself thinking of people in terms of *drivers* and *others*. Who's going to drive the creative process for this client, and who is simply going to contribute her or his role to the team?

Now understand, this was long before I became a creative thinking expert. But it was during these years of moving people around on the great game board of ad agency account teams that I first got the sense that not all people were the same kinds of creative animals. Therefore, to produce the greatest creative bounty, I needed to cultivate, or manage, these "idea creatures" differently from one to the next. I call this management process Mind Farming.

> *In the same way farmers have to manage pigs differently than cows and sheep differently than chickens, managers need to cultivate the various mind-sets of the different animals who work for them to reap the greatest results.*

THE BASICS OF MIND FARMING

Every person in your company has unlimited untapped creative thinking capabilities—more than they themselves might know exist. And the first step in developing these dormant capabil-

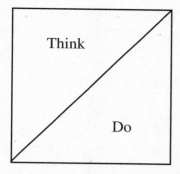

ities is to identify where people stand currently in realizing their creative thinking potential.

Let's start by making a distinction between *thinking* and *doing*, using *mind* and *body*, as those modes of working relate to the primary functions of individuals and jobs. We all think and do virtually every waking moment, even when *doing* is only sitting at a computer or sleeping. Everyone in your organization falls principally into either the thinking mode or doing mode as they provide their greatest single value to the organization. Increasingly in business, companies employ more and more people for their thinking and fewer and fewer for their doing (see the Imagination Age grid on page 16).

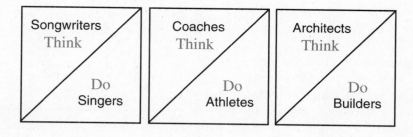

Surprisingly, thinking and doing are two concepts that are often confused when discussing creativity. Imagination, ingenuity, and innovation are, of course, all in the realm of thinking. The execution of the ideas that emerge from creative thinking is mostly in the doing realm — in which we use our eyes, hands, arms, backs, and legs.

As we discussed earlier, people often confuse these realms. "I'm not creative. I can't draw a straight line," we often hear. Or, here's another misconception: "Listen to her sing. Isn't she creative?" Not necessarily. Drawing and singing are in the doing realm, where very little creativity occurs. Songwriting, but not singing, is in the thinking realm. Drawing a straight line requires no creativity. It requires talent, maybe skill, but it's not an example of creativity because it's not thinking of something new. As we discussed in Chapter 4 our society has somehow twisted the term *creativity* to mean "artistic." Most art is the result of talent, "doing," unless it's based on an original idea, in which case it's an expression of creativity, an expression of the original idea that happened in the thinking realm. There are exceptions, such as abstract painting, where the artist "does" usually without preconceptions.

Now, all this discussion of the thinking realm forces another distinction: creative thinking versus rational thinking, or new ideas versus old ideas. As Einstein put it, imagination versus knowledge, what might be versus what is.

In the same way we need to be clear on the two modes of thinking, we need to distinguish between the two modes of doing: *crafting,* or doing with care, and *laboring,* or just knocking it out. Together, these four basic modes of function comprise the spectrum of creative thinking types within which all people function. They also denote the four basic animals that Mind Farmers must cultivate.

Let's examine these different animals and discuss the distinct dimensions that define them. For this up-close examination, we start at the bottom right of this creative typologies map, and working clockwise toward the top left, we iden-

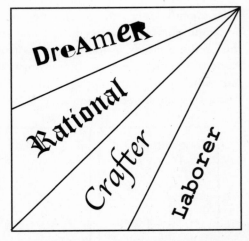

The four basic Mind Farming personality types.

Mind Farming Worksheet
for individuals on your team

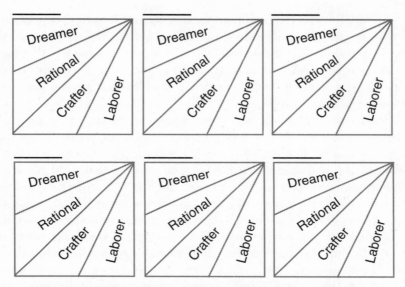

As we discuss the traits and attributes of these typologies, choose a team in your company and plot the individuals according to the Mind Farming personality types. Put the individual's initials on the blank above his or her Mind Farming map. Then circle the typology that best suits their primary contribution to the team as shown on the example below. (Please note that functional teams tend to be no more than six to eight people.)

Example:

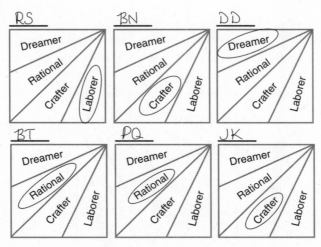

tify the *laborer*, the *crafter*, the *rational*, and the *dreamer*. The first two are principally in the doing mode, of course, and the latter two are in the thinking mode.

All individuals function in all four fields at different points in time, as they migrate around the map according to what they're doing or the challenges that face them. But all individuals also have a dominant thinking mode and a dominant doing mode, one of which is their superdominant mode, which normally defines that person's primary value to the organization.

Sometimes you can be in all four modes over a very short period of time. Let's take the example of painting your living room. When considering unusual paint colors, say periwinkle or puce, or trying to match color on the underside of a rubber plant leaf, you would be in the *dreamer mode*. When considering colors such as tan or gray, colors that are more common, you would be in the *rational mode*. When doing the fine work of painting—cutting edges or painting a window sash—you'd be in what I term the *crafter mode*. But when you're watching something on TV or doing something else that occupies your mind while at the same time painting the walls (barely concentrating on what you're doing), then in terms of Mind Farming you're in the *laborer mode*.

THE LABORER MODE

Those who operate entirely or mostly in the laborer mode are the foundation of the doing workforce. Since the beginning of time, most organizations have needed laborers, but this demand has been decreasing recently as machines and computers take over many of the

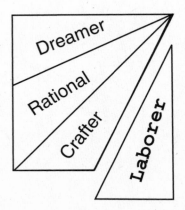

predominantly physical-labor-intensive jobs and repetitive, routine functions.

❧❖❧

TYPICAL CAREER LABORER JOBS

- Data entry
- Cab drivers
- Bank tellers
- Ditch diggers
- Toll takers

Temporary laborers:

- Juniors/trainees

---------------------------- ❖ ----------------------------

Laborers are most often the less career-minded side of the doing workforce. These same doers who have upward mobility on their minds or who take jobs as a temporary means to an end are not permanent members of this typology (e.g., the student just out of school, the actor who waits on tables). Even the most creative minds—rocket scientists, for example—while mowing the lawn on their off-hours, enjoy periods in this no-brainer mode.

Career laborers, those who function principally in the laborer mode with little intention of moving higher in the creative thinking hierarchy, most often need to be told what to do, as well as how, when, and where to do it. And they routinely need someone else to supervise them, to tell them whether they've done their jobs properly and when they are finished. These hard-core laborers tend to do only what it takes to get the job done; they're often in no particular hurry, and, should a problem occur, it's usually their nature to wait for others to solve it. They may tend to leave at 5:00 sharp, whether or not the job has been completed.

THE CRAFTER MODE

The crafters also operate mainly in the doing mode, but the principal distinction here is that they take greater *care* in their jobs and, for the

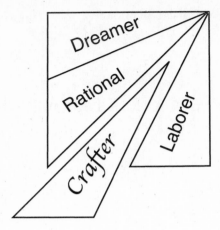

most part, can supervise themselves as they go about their doing. What keeps them mainly on the doing side of the line is that they are most often executing other people's ideas.

Crafters tend to be precise, reliable, responsible, and patient. They will be found working past 5:00 if necessary to properly complete the job.

⚜

TYPICAL CRAFTER JOBS

- Mechanics
- Word processors
- Musicians
- Flight attendants
- Photographers

❖

This typology likely comprises the more career-minded, quality-oriented segment of the doer workforce, as well as their lower-level supervisors and other professionals who are principally doers.

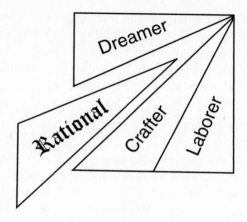

THE RATIONAL MODE

The first of the two thinking modes comprise the rationals. When we operate as rationals we're operating principally in the known. In the more mundane aspects of this mode, we are often performing routine mental tasks. On the more developed end of the rational spectrum, we are solving problems by finding solutions in the known, that is, ours and others' experiences, the tried-and-true. Those who function much of the time in this mode must have a great deal of knowledge and experience to draw upon in order to find solutions. They tend to be somewhat risk averse. Operating outside the known is not comfortable for them. And they tend to be more detail-oriented and have longer attention spans than dreamers.

❧❀❧

TYPICAL RATIONAL JOBS

You typically find the less imaginative players from the Thinking hemisphere in the following job functions:

- Loan officers
- Salespeople
- Hotel managers
- Police chiefs
- Politicians

❖

Rational dominants comprise the less imaginative thinking workforce, and for that reason, those who function only in the rational mode rarely stretch to create solutions beyond the known and are therefore often the lower-achieving members of the thinking strata.

Most people in business are rational dominant.

THE DREAMER MODE

People whose primary value to the organization is contributing new ideas are the dreamers. Those who primarily function in the dreamer mode are most often fully capable of finding solutions in the rational mode but would rather explore the great unknown, thinking creatively to see if there might be a better solution that hasn't yet been tried.

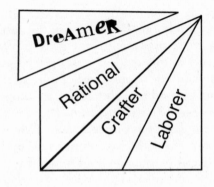

TYPICAL DREAMER JOBS

- Scientists
- Leading songwriters
- Leading engineers
- R&D people
- Leading doctors

It can be said that dreamers are quite curious by nature. They have active minds, always considering many solutions to problems, always trying different ideas on for size. Dreamers love to take a fresh perspective on things, are open-minded, and often have very short attention spans, moving on to the next thing even before their creative ideas have been executed, often leaving that to others.

Leonardo da Vinci often functioned in the dreamer mode, wondering why water speeds up when flowing around rocks in a river and how to use that dynamic for mechanical purposes, or pondering the makeup of sunlight and how to capture and use it. But his short attention span also led to many partially completed projects, and da Vinci upset more than one monastery by leaving ambitious but only half-finished murals in his wake.

A Note of Caution

Making broad generalizations and pigeonholing people has its limitations, particularly when trying to help people grow professionally and personally. I have serious reservations about typecasting people for life. If Hollywood had pegged Leslie Nielson only as a bad guy and never given him the opportunity to show his lighter side, we would not be the beneficiaries of one of the funnier actors of the big screen in the past 20 years. If baseball had kept Babe Ruth as the pitcher he started out to be, and he played in only every fourth or fifth game (as pitchers traditionally do), "America's greatest pastime" would have been cheated out of one of its great batting heroes.

That said, if we are, in fact, trying to develop certain propensities (or lack thereof, as the case may be) in people, then it definitely does make sense to identify and better understand the starting point.

It's also important to note that we are attempting to identify the dominant and superdominant personality types as they relate to an individual's vital role on a particular team. If a person is a highly developed crafter in one area of his or her life, that does not necessarily translate to all areas of life.

We have all seen the sharp, task-oriented middle manager (rational/crafter) fail miserably when promoted to an upper management role where dreamer traits are in greater demand.

Other personality traits can sometimes override an individual's natural mode in a Mind Farming sense. I've had more than one creative or client service executive work for me who was an absolute star with regard to ongoing client business, but just couldn't perform anywhere near their potential in the pressure cooker of new business. Conversely, I have had people who perform at their best under intense pressure and

Mind Farming Team Worksheet

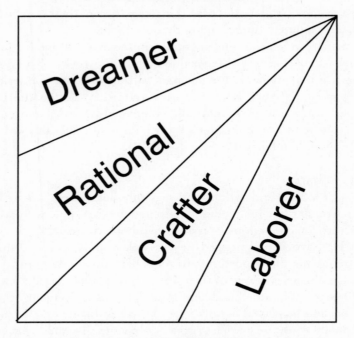

Here I'll ask you to create a composite of the individual Mind Farming maps you did on page 189. Simply enter the initials of each person from their individual score sheets into the appropriate quadrant on the team worksheet. If you take the example worksheet on page 189 and transfer those typologies, it would look like this:

Example:

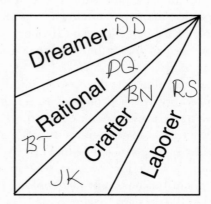

were brought in expressly for that role (similar to the third-down back in football).

BEWARE THE PHANTOM

Some people are not who they appear to be if you don't look deep enough. There's the phantom dreamer, who has had a big idea or two, often early in her or his career, and has been emulating her- or himself ever since. That person is now probably a rational. Most business people are rational dominants.

Among the most misidentified types I see in the business world are individuals who fall into a category I call "the hyperrational." A hyperrational is a person who has many, many ideas but they aren't truly original. Frankly, most people I see in business who are identified as being "very creative" by their superiors fall into this category. Very few people are *primarily* dreamers, whose main value to the organization is coming up with truly new ideas and who actually deliver them.

WHY WE NEED TO DEVELOP ALL SECTORS

If you haven't yet taken my Creative IQ Test for Organizations, and if you have not yet done a quick Creative ForceField Analysis, I suggest you do so now to make the rest of this chapter more meaningful.

Dramatic Shifts in Makeup of Workforce

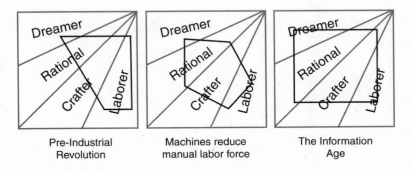

| Pre-Industrial Revolution | Machines reduce manual labor force | The Information Age |

Our need for Laborers has decreased over the years, as our need for Rationals and Dreamers has increased.

> *Although most organizations need players at all positions on the Mind Farming map, never has there been such an urgent need to develop creativity in all types of individuals.*

First, with the flatter organizational structure of most companies today, with more expected of everyone, we need people to function as fully and as independently as possible as frequently as possible. Also, as the breakneck pace of change brings virtually constant challenges and problems to be solved, we need more and more nimble minds in our organizations to help us thrive, or at least remain competitive.

There are some basic things management can do to develop all people in their organizations, thinkers as well as doers, to be more creative thinkers.

Challenge Your People

One of the reasons many people in business underachieve is because they are simply not challenged. If creative thinking is the same thing as problem solving, as we discussed in Chapter 2, then people who are forced to stretch to create solutions where none can be found in the known invariably come up with some new ideas. Or at least they try. The human spirit, almost by nature, is curious. Give them a challenge and let them know their ideas will be considered, seriously considered, and you might be surprised to see how many people rise to the occasion.

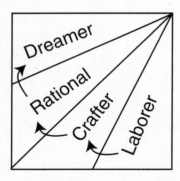

There has always been a natural progression, as laborers become crafters, and crafters become thinkers and managers as their careers progress.

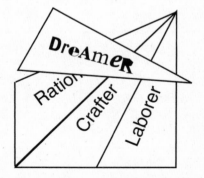

Today, however, we need people at all levels to have the dreamer traits of open-mindedness, the ability to change and "create" solutions to the constant flow of new problems.

I have worked with many top management teams who complain that their underlings rarely offer fresh ideas, yet those at the top often fail to see their own reluctance to accept challenges as the reason the next level contributes so little in this area.

Provide Lots of Encouragement

Look at the word *encouragement*. The root, of course, is *courage*. It takes guts to come up with new ideas. And even more guts to say them aloud. "What if I'm wrong?" "What if no one likes it?" "What if it fails?" These are strong emotional reactions, to be sure.

To induce your people to explore the great unknown, with few assurances of which ideas will work, requires a great deal of encouragement on the part of management. And what's the opposite of encouragement? Discouragement, right? The quick-on-the-trigger manager who instantly judges an employee's idea to be less than wonderful once too often (which might be only once if done too harshly) may provide all the discouragement that individual needs to remain a crafter or rational the rest of his or her professional life, robbing the organization of a potentially powerful resource.

Consciously provide encouragement, and consciously refrain from discouragement. And insist that your top managers do so as well. You'll be fostering an environment in which people will volunteer ideas to make your products and services, and all aspects of your company, better and better and better.

One simple tactic I have used as a manager when trying to get people to stretch creatively is to say, "I know you can do better than this." If I instead said, "This isn't good," or even, "This isn't there yet," I may sound more discouraging than is necessary.

Give People Freedom

Another way to develop creative thinkers and problem solvers in your organization is to give your people freedom. Lots of it. Freedom to think beyond the known, the tried-and-true. And, perhaps more important, you must give your people freedom to fail.

Few people like to fail. Yet there are organizations, even industries, where failure is accepted, even encouraged. Engineering and science are two fields where failure is simply a part of the exploration process in problem solving.

One of the most overpromised, underdelivered practices I see in my consulting work is this so-called freedom to fail. It's easy for many managers to give it lip service, but when failure happens, it's often very difficult for them to live up to their words. It may be trite, but people follow the lead of what you *do*, not what you say.

Understanding Is the Key

To develop as creative thinkers in your organization, first your people have to understand that creative thinking is the most important weapon your company has in the battle to compete in the rough-and-tough, even hostile world of business. Your people need to know that creative thinking and problem solving are fundamental to virtually everything else they do in all realms of their particular jobs.

There is another kind of understanding that can help your people become great achievers in this area. And that is their understanding of how to come up with ideas — basic creative thinking and problem solving.

Of course, the primary objective of this book is to provide understanding of this elusive stuff called *creativity*. As we demonstrated earlier, everyone has the capability to come up with ideas and solve problems. Yet, do they get the big idea, the big solution, every time? No. Actually, most people are quite inconsistent in doing so. And the reason for this is quite simple. Most people have no idea *how* they come up with ideas or solve problems, so replicating it consistently is quite difficult for them.

A METHOD TO THE MADNESS

If you study the traits of real-life dreamers, the most fully developed thinkers on the creative typologies map, you will see some similarities. From Albert Einstein to Stephen Hawking, from Leonardo da Vinci to Martha Graham, from Thomas Edison to Steve Jobs, from Mozart to the Beatles . . . all of these great, leading-edge thinkers have some fundamental characteristics that actually can be developed in anyone.

I have worked for years to identify definitive creative thinker traits. I've trained over 100,000 individuals, many of them dreamers who want to be even better dreamers, the vast majority of whom are crafters and rationals, and even some laborers (often dragged kicking and screaming to the training sessions by their bosses). During my training sessions — some that last only one hour, most in the half- to full-day range, some that last for three days — virtually all participants become consistent, effective dreamers, proving that anyone can improve the ability to think more creatively if given a better understanding and the proper conditions.

The thinking methods featured in this book, 100 MPH Thinking, Intergalactic Thinking, 180° Thinking, and so on, have been designed to help all individuals access their dreamer mode. Although the creative thinking skills I help people develop are quite simple and easy to learn and use, the biggest challenge is in getting people to let go of the belief that "creativity is for the chosen few" and the lifelong hit-or-miss habits they use in problem solving. Most of these habits are learned only through blind experimentation, with no real certainty of success at any given time.

The three principal creative thinking traits around which I build my training have already been mentioned as the three defining characteristics of dreamers: curiosity, an active mind, and a fresh perspective. See below how my major Do-It-Yourself Lobotomy tools match up to stimulate these three vital creative thinking traits.

How to Develop Curiosity

The creative thinking power tool that can be used to stimulate the same kind of curiosity that natural dreamers seem to possess in such great quantity is what I call Ask a Better Question.

Simply by stating your problem or objective in the form of a question, you start the mental wheels turning, thus priming the imagination. Human beings are quite curious by nature. Whereas fully developed dreamers seem to be curious about almost everything and are never satisfied with things even if they seem to work quite well, the rest of us can prompt that inquisitive mind quite simply by asking a question. And the better the question, the more we stimulate our natural curiosity.

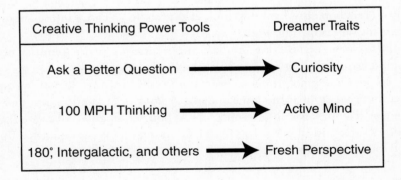

Creative Thinking Power Tools	Dreamer Traits
Ask a Better Question ⟶	Curiosity
100 MPH Thinking ⟶	Active Mind
180°, Intergalactic, and others ⟶	Fresh Perspective

Let's say an airline company challenges its ground service and flight crews by asking them to find ways to improve on-time departure by 10 percent. That question will stimulate many new ideas in people, as they examine the departure procedures, determine what causes delays, and apply some good old-fashioned ingenuity to solve the problem. And if they do a good job, they just might reach their 10 percent improvement goal.

But let's also say that the airline's competitor has asked its people, "How can we improve our departure record by 50 percent?" Just by asking a better question, the second airline has triggered more curiosity. Employees in the second company will probably consider some of the same improvement measures as those in the first airline, but they will also strive well beyond the first team—not just looking for marginal improvement but for paradigm-shifting changes—simply by asking what some engineers I once worked with call a "stretch question."

How to Develop Active Minds

Nurturing active minds is as much a part of developing a corporate mind-set as thinking habits and practices. Developing a corporate mind-set starts at the top of the company and within each department, and it is critical to long-term success on this front. Are the leaders in your company dreamers? They need to be if they are to truly lead your company past the competition and into a bright future.

As for the pure mechanics of an active mind, how do you get people to come up with more ideas? One simple way is to actually keep score. "I'd like to see 50 new ways to capitalize on this opportunity," you might say when soliciting some solutions. You can further push your people by challenging them: "Make sure you have your 200 outtakes within reach in case I want to look at the 'chaff.'" That kind of encouragement will certainly do it.

Also, when conducting brainstorming sessions, make quantity your goal, not quality. The quality will take care of itself.

Expect many solutions to even the smallest of problems. Develop this thinking style at the lowest levels in your organization, not just at the top. Tomorrow's thought leaders in your company will come from today's rank and file. My 100 MPH Thinking tool is particularly effective for activating minds.

HOW TO DEVELOP FRESH PERSPECTIVE

Developing people with perpetually fresh viewpoints is also something that starts at the top in a well-run organization. If managers aren't generating, or at least open to hearing, new ideas, how can an organization expect to develop this type of mentality in the rest of its people? If a company doesn't accept a degree of failure from those who are trying to push the envelope, how can they expect to explore new frontiers?

To push freshness of thought, encourage your people to practice Intergalactic Thinking and 180° Thinking consciously and purposefully, both in groupthink and individually. But, remember, if management doesn't manage for greater creativity and isn't open to the new ideas that emerge, little progress will be made on this front.

THE KEYS TO CREATIVITY ARE IN THE CORNER OFFICE

I'll end this chapter by telling you about an exercise I use to wind up my Mind Farming workshops.

Toward the end of the program, I divide the group into four segments. I give each segment virtually the same assignment posed four different ways. After they complete this short drill, I have all participants share their results. Here's what happens every time. Group A is consistently more creative than groups B, C, and D. Group B is invariably the next most creative. Group C typically comes in third. And those pathetic guinea pigs in group D unfailingly come in last. Why? Because I manage them into increasingly tighter limits on their creativity.

With all due respect for the "natural tendencies" of people revealed in our discussion of the Mind Farming personalities (dreamers, rationals,

That big idea you had last year is still impacting the company's bottom line. Can you spell promotion?

Timeline of a great idea (continued)

Timeline of a lousy idea (continued)

crafters, and laborers), the makeup of subsegments I include in my little exercise is irrelevant. I manage all people in group A to be dreamers. I manage all individuals in the B group to be rationals, and so on
down the food chain.

> *It's that simple: Manage for creativity and you will get creativity. Put
> the lid on creativity and it will wither away like a beautiful flower
> locked in the basement.*

You are the Mind Farmer; it's entirely up to you.

Cheat Notes for Chapter 18: Mind Farming

- *People are different animals; their creativity needs to be cultivated differently.*

- *Everyone falls principally into either the "thinking" modes of rationals or dreamers, or the "doing" modes of crafters or laborers.*

- *All individuals have a dominant thinking mode and a dominant doing mode, one of which is their superdominant mode, which normally defines that person's primary value to the organization.*

- *Management can do some basic things to develop creative thinkers: Provide challenges, encouragement, freedom, and understanding.*

- *The Do-It-Yourself Lobotomy thinking tools stimulate the primary traits of creative thinking: curiosity, active mind, and fresh perspective.*

- *Manage for creativity and you will get creativity. Put the lid on creativity and you rob your organization of a valuable resource.*

Storming the Brain

Opening one's own mind to find truly new ideas, concepts that have never been discovered before, can be a challenge, but the rewards are certainly worth the effort. There has always been and always will be all kinds of forces working against new ideas. Yet creative thinking is increasingly called for in business today, so it simply must be done to grease the skids of progress.

Of course, that's what this book is all about—helping you, as an individual, become a better creative thinker. All the chapters to this point have been aimed at increasing your ability to come up with great, fresh ideas when you need them, with the exception, of course, of the previous chapter, which focused on cultivating fresh thinking in others.

But let me tell you in no uncertain terms:

> *It's one thing to be a creative thinker and it's quite another thing altogether to inspire an entire roomful of people to be fresh thinkers.*

This is a process most commonly referred to as *brainstorming, ideation,* and *groupthink.* I'll use those terms interchangeably in this chapter, with brainstorming carrying most of the load. I want to tell you that brainstorming is an entirely different kettle of fish, and they just might be sharks.

The first thing I'll point out about brainstorming is how amazingly ill understood this process is. When we go into companies, my fellow

Do-It-Yourself Lobotomy coaches and I see so many poor excuses for brainstorming techniques, it's no wonder there's a rolling brownout of creativity in business today.

GREAT MINDS don't THINK ALIKE

In 1998, I was leading a brainstorming session for Sears in one of its major foreign markets. We were trying to come up with a "millennium idea"—you know, a big PR, community-serving concept that would be executed within the millennium context.

We had 35 people from the Sears marketing team and a few dozen assorted dummies assembled for brainstorming. (Maybe I need to explain this a bit more. We held the session in a very cool environment for brainstorming, a retail display warehouse with, among other things, over a hundred mannequins. Sorry if I misled you.)

We arranged our 35 people in groups of 5 in various corners of a large room. One of our ground rules was that if more than one group came up with an idea, it was immediately thrown out.

People often use duplication as validation of brilliance. "Great minds think alike." But the truth is that great minds have *different* ideas. The great unwashed masses are the ones who think alike.

If the Sears millennium team found duplication with only 35 people, weren't the chances high that the idea would be developed by their competition?

❖

We see too many people in the room. We see too few people in the room. We see processes that are billed as creative thinking sessions that look more like Nazi Youth Camps. We see methods that are better suited to tarring and feathering new ideas than discovering and nurturing them. We see dominant managers organizing groups under the guise of brainstorming, meetings that are nothing more than manipulation sessions to get the whole group to agree with the leader's preconceptions.

Brainstorming is a process with a lot of faces, and I must tell you that most of them are as ugly as a maggot under a microscope.

To someone like me, a person who eats, breathes, sings, and yodels creative thinking, going into these types of environments is like Mother Teresa walking into a bordello on New Year's Eve. Then again, these companies have called us for our expertise. So maybe they know they are way off base in this process. (I can only imagine how messed up some of the companies who *don't* call in the creative medics might be.)

"Okay, smarty brainstorming guru," you ask, "if we're doing it all wrong, then why don't you share some of your wisdom and tell us how it is done?" (See, I know so much about the human mind, I know exactly what you are thinking.)

THE DO'S AND DON'TS OF BRAINSTORMING

Well, to be honest with you, if I tried to cover everything I know about brainstorming in these pages, that chapter alone would be larger than this entire book. But I can give you a quick list of do's and don'ts that I'm sure will shed a good deal of light on this murky, misunderstood process.

Do: Set aside at least two hours (I prefer three) to make sure you get beyond the surface in your thinking.

Don't: Expect to blast in and find the holy grail of answers after taking a few minutes to just scratch the epidermal layer of thought.

Do: Invite 20 to 30 people to the meeting. The more people, the more ideas — to a point.

Don't: Expect three or four people to provide the energy, momentum, or mental leverage to make big leaps, or you'll be very disappointed.

Do: Invite a wide array of people to participate in your brainstorming session. The broader the cross section of players, the wider the variety of ideas.

Don't: Expect a group of people closely associated with the area being brainstormed to be the most freethinking bunch. In areas such as new product exploration, I often convince clients to keep their people out of the room altogether and assemble a group of customers or potential users of the product in question. The further away the participants are from the realities of marketing, the less encumbered the players are by what can and can't be done. Some great ideas have been discovered by people who didn't know "it couldn't be done."

Do: Divide the group into smaller teams of four to six people so you get more diverse thought and to dilute the negative impact of the troublemakers. (I sometimes identify the know-it-alls in advance and stick them in the same group to duke it out.)

Don't: Put eight or more people on one team. If you have eight people, have two groups of four. This is the biggest mistake groups make. (Too many cooks do not make creative soup; they make only a watered-down concoction we've all tasted before.)

Do: Some kind of a little creative thinking warm-up to help break the ice. Make sure the warm-up has nothing to do with the topic to be brainstormed. People are less self-conscious coming up with new ideas in areas where they have less attachment. The freethinking here will help them loosen up for the main event.

Don't: Just start people off on a grueling thinking adventure without stretching their mental muscles and loosening them up.

Do: Your brainstorming in bursts. Spend 20 minutes looking for ideas *this* way, then 20 minutes doing it *that* way. (This is a good place to use Intergalactic Thinking, using different galaxies for each burst of effort.)

Don't: Try to make the group chase after the prize without pacing themselves. People are much better running lots of small sprints than one long marathon.

Do: Have people jot down their own ideas (see "Jotting," page 143). I like the standard size sticky notes because they're small (you can't get too verbose in a 3" × 3" space) and modular, so you can move them around during the distillation process, like

---

The Lobotomy Files

Three-Ring Brainstorming

When we conduct a brainstorming session using the Do-It-Yourself Lobotomy techniques, it's as if the circus has come to town. Before you know it our stodgy analyticals are flying like the trapeze artists, our grumpy, "that-won't-work" crowd is clowning around, and the aloof are clamoring to get a ride on the elephants and camels. This process helps bring out the best thinking in a group. And there are some real winners among the hundreds or even thousands of ideas generated.

Mike A. Ricciuto
Director, Global Communications
DuPont Crop Protection
Lobotomized 1999

pieces on a game board, and you don't have to waste time transcribing.

Don't: Have one person be a scribe. It eliminates that person's full
involvement and sometimes diffuses the ownership of an idea
that may later need a champion to keep it alive.

Do: Ask people to stand while they are ideating. People actually
think better when they are standing. Cross-lateral activity such
as walking, jogging, swimming, and biking stimulates the brain.
Standing still is actually not an inert state at all, but a constant
balancing act using cross-lateral muscle activity. I like to use
pads on easels for posting the sticky notes with ideas written on
them, or use the sheets from such pads taped to the wall. I also
like to keep chairs at a distance to avoid the temptation to sit. Of
course, pregnant women and octogenarians are excluded from
the rule.

Don't: Have people sit comfortably around a table unless you're
willing to supply a steady stream of coffee or pillows.

Do: Ask all players to say their ideas aloud as they write them
down. It cross-pollinates the other players on their team and
contributes to a level of chatter that gives the team some energy.
When all teams are thinking out loud it adds group energy that
is both competitive and supportive for the entire room.

Don't: Ask people to remain silent for most of the session. This can
contribute to very low energy. There are times, however, when I
ask teams or the entire room to spend, say, 5 or 10 minutes ideating in silence. I do this when I feel the group has been distracted
from the main mission by digression or judgment, or even when
the energy is getting low. Regarding that last point, rather than
allowing low energy to be a negative element of the atmosphere,
sometimes it's easier to go with the flow than to fight it and lose.

Do: Change the dynamics throughout the session. Push the group's
thinking first this way, then that way, then some other way. Off-
center methods of thinking can become routine very quickly.

Don't: Keep pushing in the same direction. Creative thinking means
finding surprising answers. You can't keep looking in the same
place or in the same way and expect to find something different.

Do: Use toys, props, music, anything to alter the ambience, tone,
and tempo. I like rock 'n' roll blasting one minute, classical
music the next. I also use crayons, food, and games.

Don't: Expect a boring atmosphere to lead to exciting results.

Scientific discovery:
Neckties don't inhibit creativity.

Have you
ever heard,
when typical
b u s i n e s s
p e o p l e
want to be
"creative,"
" W e ' r e
going off
site. And
no ties."*†
Okay, I buy
some of this.
The team will
be putting in
some heavy
thinking. So we'll
get out of the
office. (Not such a
bad idea. Change
of environment.)
But no ties? (Excuse
me?) So it's neckties
that have been in-
hibiting creativity in
business all of these
years? I don't think so.
Documented, the most
creative thinker ever in
American history, Thomas
Edison (with 1,093 patents),
wore a tie to work every day.
I mean, he even wore a tie to
sleep. That is, he napped
often during the day and didn't
always take off his signature
bow tie during nappy time. Well,
Edison's habits are scientific
enough for me to conclude
that neckties do not, I
repeat, "do not" in-
hibit creativity.
Do you get
my poi-
nt
?

* Hint of sexism noted, with a hint of apology.
† For our readers from California, a necktie is an article of clothing
often worn by businessmen and by disgruntled teens at funerals.

Do: Find an interesting venue for the session. I like nature and kid-oriented locations; country clubs, yacht clubs, theme parks, children's museums, and such.

Don't: Book a room at the local chain hotel with the same carpeting as the last 10 meetings, and don't expect unusual thinking to soar in the company conference room.

Do: Keep pushing for quantity (see Chapter 7, "100 MPH Thinking"). Quality will surface.

Don't: Try to find *the* perfect idea. That's very hard to do, and it encourages too much judgment too soon.

Do: Distill the output periodically. When each group has 30, 40, 50 ideas, have them distill the field down to the cream and start another round.

Don't: Build up a huge mass of ideas that will be impossible to get your mind around to condense later.

WHICH IS *THE* IDEA?

As hard as it can be to get to a mass of great ideas, whether in group brainstorming or on your own, it can be even more difficult to whittle down that mass to *the* single most definitive answer, or even to a manageable shortlist.

⚜

HAMBURGER OR STEAK?

I'm often asked by clients and workshop attendees, "How do we know when the creative process is finished?"

People look to me as the great creative master for such answers. My smart-ass reply is, "It's never done. You can always come up with something better. And if you don't, someone else will." There, I have the answer. I must be brilliant. No wonder they flock to me with their plebeian questions.

Well, contrary to my Mom's firmest beliefs, I'm not *always* brilliant. Case in point (actually, it's Monahan's Proven Lack-of-Brilliance Case #9,347): A number of years ago I was forced to sell a young pet 400-pound bull for $.50 on the hoof (don't ask). I lamented to a farmer neighbor of mine, "If I had waited a bit longer I could have sold him for $.75 per pound steak."

This Rhode Island Swamp Yankee, as we call them around these parts, gave me that patented Yankee look. All that was missing was the corncob pipe. Then he said, "Should have sold him 100 pounds ago, when he was $1.00 a pound veal."

Yes, you can overwork an idea. Yes, you can often go with an earlier idea. But in matters of creativity, unlike the cattle business, you should generate many ideas. Then you *can* go back and find the veal. The prime cut of veal, at that.

❖

Here are some tips on how to get there from here.

Distill periodically. As mentioned earlier, don't wait until the end to try to sort through the output of an entire brainstorming session. Being forced to evaluate each idea a number of times, once during the round-by-round distillation and again during the semifinal and final rounds, helps you look at it in different lights to truly test the idea in its conceptual form. Also, because the early distillation is understood not to be binding and allows for inclusion of what may be seen as borderline ideas early on, it keeps final, more destructive judgment at bay.

Don't debate during the early stages of distillation. During the early rounds you can distill simply by asking all members of the team (the four- to six-member group, not the entire room) to nominate ideas for that team's shortlist. If you're using sticky notes, this simply means moving the sticky to the shortlist. If one person likes an idea enough to put it in the running, then it's in the running. By saving the oral arguments for later, you're keeping everyone in an open mind-set. Debate causes both defenders and attackers to take a stand, one that they may become attached to later; this almost always clouds their judgment.

Bring some criteria to the qualifying process. In addition to deferring the intellectual discussion of why an idea is good or bad until late in the

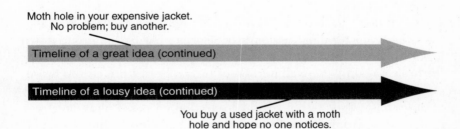

process, it's a good idea to save qualifying criteria until later as well. When you announce the criteria by which the final idea(s) will be chosen too early (some groups do this at the beginning), you narrow the playing field too soon. Remember what we said about planning and getting attached to the outcome and how it limits the possibilities? Well, articulating the success criteria too soon not only limits possibilities, but it also tends to eliminate that valuable fertilizer that is so crucial to the creative process.

Bringing criteria into the process when final or near-final judgments are being made also eliminates much of the subjectivity from the evaluation. It become less a matter of whether people like it or don't like it (which you can never fully eliminate, nor do you want to), and more an exercise of whether it fits the bill or not. This keeps the process less personal. It's hard to make a subjective judgment on an idea and not offend the person who thought of it.

Use numeric scoring. When getting to the short strokes, I like to use a silent voting system. Again, you eliminate debate, which is rarely a fair fight between people of differing ranks, and you make the process more quantitative, which brings in a little, not a lot, of science. The simplest numeric scoring system is to allot each player on the team a finite number of votes, which I do by simply having the individuals place a checkmark on the sticky note where the idea is written.

Let's say we have five players on a team with five votes each. That puts 25 points into play. Ask people not to be persuaded nor dissuaded by one another's votes. Then simply rank finalist ideas according to the math. In this example, the highest score could be a five, the lowest, of course, is zero. Afterward, I ask people to rearrange the stickies with the highest-scoring ideas on the top of the page. This usually results in a pyramidal effect, with people agreeing on just a few ideas at the top, which is most often a fair representation of what all parties really think.

Save the final list for a later date. If at all possible, I recommend you save final judgment for a later date, if only until the following day. Even a period of as little as 24 hours will help give you a fresh, more objective perspective.

If you don't have the time, do something to change the dynamics from the brainstorming session proper. I like paring the group down for this phase. Whereas 30 to 35 people, in groups of 5 or 6, is ideal for the brains-against-the-wall portion of the process, I prefer 4 to 6 people for the final distillation.

Bring in fresh minds. For the final selection process I like some fresh perspectives. Bring in people who are not at all close to the project for the clearest opinions. This is also a good time to include people you may have liked to see participate in the brainstorming session but for some reason couldn't make it.

I also like to use fresh minds to go back to the outtake pile(s) to make sure nothing got lost between the cracks. Often some of the best ideas in a brainstorming session don't even make it out of the early rounds. If not the best ideas, they are often the freshest ideas, in part because they "didn't make sense." (See Chapter 15, page 155.)

THE BENEFITS OF CHAOS

With all the do's and don'ts and other guidelines outlined here, you may be thinking, "Boy, Monahan is proposing a lot of rules to help me break the rules."

Well, you've pretty much figured out the method to the madness.

> *When left to their own devices, most people use little discipline in their creative thinking, only to yield totally predictable results.*

This is particularly true of groupthink. This chapter (in fact, the entire book) is aiming to impose an order—or, perhaps better stated, "ordered disorder"—to the process to better ensure a less predictable outcome.

When I run a brainstorming session it is my objective to create such a discord of thinking that it causes participants to be constantly off balance. I look to constantly create an effect not unlike the first shot in billiards when all balls scatter every which way, when anything can happen, and something often does. When most people think through an issue, it's more like calling a shot, lining it up and sinking it, which might be good when shooting pool, but it's the worst way to try to find a new idea.

At one session I ran a few years ago to brainstorm a new name for a company, we had the typical chaos, the antithesis of Robert's Rules that characterizes the groupthink meetings I conduct. In a session like this, there can be only one winning ideating team. However, afterward an executive came up to me and said, "Everyone's happy. They all think it's *their* idea," implying that the chaos had an unexpected benefit.

Sometimes to keep your thinking unpredictable you need to create a little orderly chaos. I say, do whatever it takes to get to fresh ideas. The rewards are worth it.

Cheat Notes for Chapter 19:
Storming the Brain

- *Allow enough time to get beyond the surface in your thinking.*

- *Shoot for 20 to 30 participants total. A large (but not too large) group yields more ideas.*

- *Divide this group into teams of four to six people for more diverse thought and to dilute the impact of those who "know all the answers."*

- *Invite a wide variety of people to participate, and go outside the core group.*

- *Do a warm-up mental exercise to break the ice.*

- *Brainstorm in bursts; people are much better in many small sprints than in one long marathon.*

- *Have everyone jot down their own ideas on sticky notes.*

- *Ask people to stand while they are ideating.*

- *Keep pushing for quantity, and quality will surface.*

- *Distill the output periodically. Don't wait until the end.*

The Five Greatest Barriers to Creativity

A very big part of achieving your creative potential is increasing the things that lead to creative realization. Broadly speaking, those things include better understanding of this magical stuff and greater command of the actual thinking skills that lead to fresh ideas. For the most part, those two areas of concentration have been the focus of this book to this point.

If you have filled out your Creative ForceField in the Appendix, you've discovered that increasing your creative effectiveness also means diminishing the forces that work against your creative effort. (If you have not yet filled out the Creative ForceField on page 255, I suggest you do it now.)

In analyzing hundreds of these Creative ForceField forms, I've discovered some common barriers that exist for the vast majority of people in business. Here I speak to the larger blocks to help you better understand this aspect of creativity, because you can't fix what you don't understand.

BARRIER #1: FEAR OF THE UNKNOWN

Fear comes out in a lot of different ways relative to creativity. Just exploring new ideas brings on fear because new ideas are part of the great unknown. New ideas aren't proven. Maybe it's just human nature to fear the unknown, but it's certainly a pattern that's been with us for centuries.

In the early days of maps, what was shown on the outer fringe of the known world? Sea dragons and monsters, right? Because no one knew what was out there, they feared it.

New ideas are, by definition, unknown. One can even argue that this fear thing, a barrier for most people, is also an acid test of a new idea. I'll go even further and add that a new idea, by definition, must have some element of fear, because a new idea is unproven and therefore you might fail. So it might be a monster, but you don't know.

> *Of course, in this ever changing world, just staying with what you're doing now — not changing, not thinking of a new idea — could doom you to failure as well.*

But for some reason we find more security and less fear in the known than in the unknown.

Fear is an integral part of the creative process. What exactly are we afraid of? Well, for one thing, people simply fear being wrong. The fear of failure prevents many people from venturing, from exploring, or from taking action once they think of a new idea. But there's a paradox here. Are you aware that highly successful people fail more than average people?

Did you know that Babe Ruth not only hit more home runs than anyone else in his time, but also struck out more than anyone else in his time? One of his modern-day equivalents, Michael Jordan, missed more shots during his playing time than anyone else. I tracked this at the NBA web site for three years in a row, Michael's last three years with the Chicago Bulls, during the league championship series. Not only was Michael Jordan named MVP all three years, but he also missed more shots than anyone else. In fact, he went out in style: In his final year he missed twice as many shots as anyone else. Yet he was a winner. Albert Einstein said, "Show me someone who hasn't failed, and I'll show you someone who hasn't tried hard enough."

A study by a major university in California showed that the top scientists in the world fail more than average scientists.

We learn from failure. There is progress in failure. And not doing anything sometimes constitutes failure.

The only way to succeed is to do something, so we have to be willing to risk failure. Hockey great Wayne Gretzky says, "You miss 100 percent of the shots you don't take." We have to be willing to risk failure, because inaction is failure when it comes to things creative.

BARRIER #2: FEAR OF LOOKING STUPID

There's something else that we fear, sometimes even more than failure. And that is the fear of "what they'll think" about our idea. Our only consolation is that we are their "they" when they're fearing what others think.

But this fear is nothing to be scoffed at; it prevents people from taking a leap. I can see the apprehension around a new idea in the work I do with businesspeople every week. Often they look at a new idea, then think, "Hmm, *they're* not going to like it. *I* might look like an idiot. I might lose my job. How am I going to pay the mortgage? I'm going to have to move my family under the viaduct." It's an eight-second thought chain that leads from "they might not like it" to "life under the viaduct." Why risk it?

Why? Because you have to risk it in order to succeed.

One of the benefits of the methods we're covering in this book is that failure is built into your creative processes. You're allowed to fail. If you're doing 100 MPH Thinking and come up with 50 ideas, you could fail 49 times and still succeed. With 180° Thinking, we're *trying* to fail; we're trying to come up with bad ideas in the name of succeeding, to loosen our brains and loosen our apprehensions.

> *Would it make you feel any better to know that some of the most highly accomplished people of all time have had the fear of looking stupid?*

One of the greatest all-time writing duos of rock 'n' roll wrote songs early in their careers using a pseudonym. Mick Jagger and Keith Richards of The Rolling Stones, often referred to as the world's greatest rock 'n' roll band, first started writing songs under the pen name of Nanker Phelge. Look on their first few records and see for yourself. Could it be that they were fearful of putting themselves out there?

The Beatles, arguably the best rock 'n' roll band of all time, were writing their own material long before they were playing it in public or recording it. There are many authors who have never sent a manuscript to a publishing house or an agent for fear of rejection, fear of failure. I confess that I myself wrote a spy novel in the mid-1980s, received two rejection letters, then put the manuscript under my bed to collect dust.

Fear of failure and re-
jection gets in the way of
great   accomplishment.
But just because you
might fail during the ideation
phase doesn't mean you necessarily have to fail in
the end. Maybe my spy novel would have been better
if I had practiced 100 MPH Thinking in coming up with
the plot, then chosen the best from among 50 plot ideas.

> Results! Why, man, I have gotten a lot of results. I know several thousand things that won't work.
>
> Thomas Edison

Failure in the conceptual phase is not failure. No high-achieving
person is without failure in the laboratory of his or her mind. But it's
only the successes we look at, the great novelists, the great playwrights
and songwriters and scientists.

BARRIER #3: JUDGMENT

Another great barrier to creative thinking is judgment. Here I'm talking about judgment of others' ideas and judgment of our own ideas.
Judging ideas during the exploration phase of the creative process is
rarely beneficial. Most often, it is very destructive—destructive to the
idea in question, destructive to the creative process, and, perhaps most
damaging, destructive to the individual whose idea is being judged. I
see many ideas stifled while they are delicate little seedlings because we
judge them too early.

FLOWER POWER

A friend of mine who grows orchids took me to his greenhouse and
showed me what looked like tens of thousands of orchids. He
explained, "I enter them in competitions and I win prizes." When I
asked which ones would be the prizewinners, he said, "I don't know.
They're all seedlings right now. If I took this one," he picked up a
beauty, "and nurtured it because this is the prettiest one now, it doesn't
guarantee it will be the prettiest one later. The ugliest one now, which
I might be tempted to throw in the trash, could turn out to be the greatest winner of all." So you see? You can't know in the fragile early
stages what might become of our seedlings of ideas. And judgment too
early can prune the best ones.

BARRIER #4: ATTACHMENT

Another great block to creativity is attachment. Attachment to the old, resistance to change, and reluctance to even explore what might be a better way of doing things. A big part of attachment is unconscious. People don't say, "I'm not going to come up with a new idea; I'm going to attach myself to the old." On the contrary. They don't even *consider* that there might be a better way of doing things.

Of course, all of this is interrelated. In my work with companies, I often find greater attachment the deeper I go into the organization. You might ask why leaders emerge as leaders. Is it because they're not attached and they have new ideas? In most cases, I believe this is so.

Those who are deep in the organization, under many layers of management, may not always be the people we're looking to for ideas and the vision to take a company forward, but their attachment to the old can be a barrier. I have seen organization after organization in which the leadership has new ideas and tries to implement them, but runs into the roadblock of attachment when the rank and file are not receptive. At the same time, please know that attachment is not the exclusive domain of the rank and file; many leaders are horribly attached.

BARRIER #5: SUCCESS

Perhaps the greatest irony surrounding creativity is that one of the major barriers to creative success is success itself—an attachment of the highest order. Time and again, I see people and companies holding onto ideas, processes, products, all manner of things that contributed to success at one time or another in their history. These things have long outlived their usefulness, but are retained simply because they were part of the success formula at one point in time.

In areas (e.g., graphic design, advertising and architecture) where personal style often defines an individual or company, this is particu-

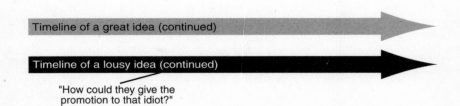

larly true. Alfred Hitchcock said that style is self-plagiarism. Many people do something great at a given point in their careers and are forever influenced by that event, either thinking they have found the creative solution that works for all situations or fearful that they'll never have such a big idea again.

The sad truth for many individuals and companies is that attachment to success heralds the beginning of the end of creative growth. The sadder truth is that more companies are forced to go out of business and more careers are derailed by people doing something they've done for years than by people doing new things. We tend to very quickly put floundering *new* companies, products, or services out of their misery compared to how slowly and reluctantly we end something that we've lived with for years, even if it is no longer relevant or serving us.

Cheat Notes for Chapter 20:
The Five Greatest Barriers to Creativity

- Fear of the unknown. *Just exploring new ideas often brings on fear because new ideas are in the great unknown.*

- Fear of looking stupid. *What will they think?*

- Judgment. *Many ideas are stifled as delicate little seedlings because we judge them too early.*

- Attachment. *Resistance to change, attachment to the old, and reluctance to even explore what might be a better way of doing things.*

- Success. *Attachment to past successes often heralds the end of creative growth.*

The Real Bibliography

The bibliography for this book has been many things: Life in general. Studying other high-achieving people. Plus a few books I've read about creativeness. A suggested reading list in the Appendix contains some very interesting material, some of which agrees with and some of which diverges from concepts in this book. Most of them are quite cogent. Creativity having the elusive nature that it does, there is certainly room for opposing viewpoints, all of which can be valid.

> *When people ask me for the titles of some good books about creativity, besides the usual reading list (see page 258) I often recommend biographies.*

Biographies are about high-achieving people. You very rarely have to worry about picking up a biography about a complete loser. Maybe there are some autobiographies in that area, I'm not sure. Biographies generally deliver more than just life stories of high-achieving people. I find that high-achieving people tend to be pretty conscious of what they do and how they do it and are therefore often good teachers. Everyone has brilliant ideas from time to time. Those who consistently have brilliant ideas are frequently very attuned to their own thought patterns and habits and limitations and how to get beyond their barriers to big thinking. So even though you may not be interested in warfare, I highly recommend that you read the biography of Ulysses S. Grant. And even though you might not be interested in science, you may want to read a biography of Einstein. It's not that you want to repeat what they did, but that you can be inspired by their creativity and learn useful lessons from their methods.

I've been touting the value of biographies for years and recommending them to people as a source of creative inspiration. Well, my theory was tested a number of years ago when I came across a biography in a little country inn where my wife and I were staying in central Massachusetts. On the bookshelf was a biography of Ed McMahon. With all due respect to Ed McMahon, who certainly has achieved a great deal in his life, I wouldn't have thought of him necessarily as biography material. I mean, he was second banana to Johnny Carson. *Star Search*. Budweiser commercials. Do you get my point? That said, I took the book to my room and decided to delve into it. Wouldn't you know, very early in the book (around page 3) I found one of the secrets to Ed McMahon's success. It was some advice his dad had given him early on in life: "When you walk into a room, act like you belong there."

For some reason that resonated with me. When you walk into a room, act like you belong there. Then it occurred to me that my humble little ad agency in Providence, Rhode Island, which I started in 1978, had, by the mid-1980s, achieved national if not global prominence as one of the most highly awarded advertising agencies in the world. It occurred to me that an important turning point in our growth was when a young copywriter right out of school asked me, "Who's the competition?"

Here we were, a small ad agency in Providence, Rhode Island, in the shadow of Boston, which was in the shadow of Madison Avenue. We could have seen ourselves as a local agency, but we thought a little bigger, as a regional agency. When we opened our doors, we decided to compete against the largest agencies in Boston, at that time Humphrey Browning McDougall and Hill Holliday. When this wet-behind-the-ears kid asked me who the competition was, that was my answer.

Not satisfied with my answer, apparently, he said, "What about the best advertising in the world? What about the best advertising of all time?" The Doyle Dane Bernbach, the Scali, McCabe, Sloves, the Ally & Gargano stuff. Those brilliant guys in California, Chiat/Day. Those guys

"Yes, grandson, I was the one who thought
of that big idea so many years ago."

Timeline of a great idea (continued)

Timeline of a lousy idea (continued)

The Lobotomy Files

**Intergalactic Improvements
in Customer Phone Support**

We addressed an important phone support issue using Intergalactic Thinking. In the "farming galaxy" we used the crop-rotating model to inspire a concept where we train only a portion of our hundreds of phone support staff on each new consumer product release. By doing this we lowered our training costs substantially and put a specialist rather than a generalist on the end of the line.

Customer Service Executive
Major Computer Manufacturer
Lobotomized 1998

For more on Intergalactic Thinking, see Chapter 9.

in Minneapolis (where Fallon McElligott was getting started). "Aren't they the competition? Doesn't our work have to compete for the consumers' attention against the best work coming out of the best agencies? At the awards shows, isn't that the competition?" The kid got me thinking. When our little agency in Providence made that shift in our mind-set and we decided to compete at that level, when we decided to walk into that room and act like we belonged there, within two years we *were* there.

I remember in 1984, the first time we entered Communication Arts, one of the most prestigious award shows. We cracked the top 10 out of over 500 entrants from around the world. I got a phone call from Dick Coyne, the founder of *Communication Arts* and its editor and designer at the time, who said, "Who are you guys and where have you been?" Well, we're here now. We went on to have a great run for another 10 years. We walked onto the national ad scene and acted like we belonged there. We took Ed McMahon's dad's advice.

The fun postscript to this story is that, as I write this book, that snotty-nosed kid from my creative department, David Lubars, is now president of one of the world's top ad agencies, Fallon McElligott in Minneapolis. David, I'm sure, subscribes to many habits of high-achieving people. He's entered the international advertising arena and made himself a part of that in no uncertain terms.

The bottom line is this: You can be inspired by anyone, draw lessons from anywhere. And I have the utmost respect for Ed McMahon for consciously picking up such a great lesson from his dad.

Cheat Notes for Chapter 21:
The Real Bibliography

- *Life is the bibliography—be conscious, be aware.*

- *Biographies offer great reading on creativeness.*

- *Study high-achieving people. They tend to be more realized creatively.*

- *High-achieving people tend to be more conscious of their abilities and are great teachers.*

- *Readings on creativity (see the Appendix for my recommended list).*

Proceed with Passion

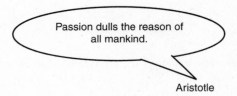

Passion dulls the reason of
all mankind.

Aristotle

I wish I could say I learned the preceding quote from my ardent study of the great philosopher's work. Alas, I must admit, I read it in a book about baseball's Boston Red Sox and their 1967 pennant drive, in which former pitching great Jim Lonborg, a legitimate intellectual in his own right, quoted the deep Greek.

"Gentleman Jim," as this Red Sox star used to be called for his mild demeanor, quoted this pithy line in an interview in the *Saturday Evening Post* in 1967 in defense of his uncharacteristic aggression on the pitching mound, throwing so close inside to batters that he actually hit them.

Passion overriding reason.

It's why otherwise good citizens loot during riots.
It accounts for many poorly matched couples who end up divorced.
It's why it's almost impossible not to pay more than you intend to at an auction.

But this passion-overriding-reason thing can also be constructive.

It's why soldiers lay down their lives for their country. (Did I say constructive?)

It's why athletes go above and beyond for the team.

It's how creative thinkers can pull out of the gravitational field of conventional thinking and dare to consider new ideas.

As we discussed earlier, new ideas don't always make a lot of sense. New ideas are often the targets for all kinds of flak. So you better have a great deal of passion in your effort to find new ideas and defend them. You're going to need it.

How do you gain and maintain the passion? Louis Armstrong, when asked by a Parisian reporter to explain American jazz, is reputed to have said, "If you gotta ask, you ain't never gonna' know."

Some people might say you either have passion or you don't.

Well, I believe everyone has a certain amount of enthusiasm for new ideas. I also believe it's easy to lose touch with that fire at the core. Our educational and societal programming has dulled much of our eagerness in this area, as has the judgment of superiors and peers and the pressure to be "right" in business.

Here are some tips to help you keep the flame burning.

Surround yourself with people who have passion for creative pursuits.

Become a student of creativeness. It is, after all, the stuff that accomplishment is made of. When my wife drags me to a ballet (sorry, Honey), I applaud the creativeness of the choreographer more than the talent of the dancers. When watching a football game, I wonder why the coach called this or that play. I don't just sit there and accept everything.

Celebrate your own successes in creative pursuits. Don't sit around waiting for the approval of others. If you have a new idea that you're excited about, don't hold back your enthusiasm. And don't listen to the naysayers. What do they know? They're the ones stuck in the old ways of thinking and attached to the old ideas.

What if Einstein had listened to the scientific community of his time? He would have thought their way and not a whole new way. What if Elvis had listened to the musical establishment, those people burning his records and calling him evil? Where would contemporary music be today?

Study, study, study. I recommend that you read about creativity and creative accomplishment as much as you can. Read books about creativity, and read as much as you can about high-achieving people. Because achievement is creativity in action.

Play in greener pastures. I heard an expression years ago. I don't know who originally said it. "If you're green, you're growing. If you're ripe, you're rotting." Put yourself in areas where you don't have all the answers so that you can wonder more, so that you can make up the answers, so that you can create.

To the latter point, how can you leverage your lessons from this book?

Practice, practice, practice. The theories and tools covered in this book might make sense as you absorb them from the comfort of your armchair. But when the heat is on to come up with a new idea, you can forget everything you've learned and revert to your defective programming if the new thinking muscles aren't in shape.

Yogi Amirit Desi, who taught me a great deal years ago, says that, according to ancient Indian understanding, ignorance does not mean acting without knowledge (how can you ignore what you never knew?), but true ignorance means having the knowledge and still ignoring it. If you hadn't understood creativity well before you read this book, then you weren't acting out of ignorance when your attachment to old ideas and old methods of thinking held you back. You just didn't know any better. If you've learned and understood the fundamentals put forth in this book and you don't lobotomize your old ideas and your old ways of thinking, then you *are* ignorant according to the ancient definition.

Use this stuff tomorrow. As with golf, tennis, or piano lessons, if you wait a few days to apply what you learned you might as well not have taken the lesson at all, because you'll remember only half of what you learned (if you're lucky). And when you wind up practicing wrong, it makes it that much harder to correct the new bad habit the next time.

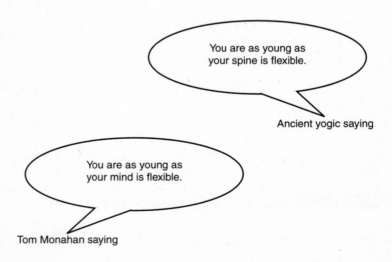

Use the cheat notes at the end of each chapter to give you the quick lowdown on the high points of each fundamental or thinking tool. I suggest you do it right now, even before you put down this book. Do one last review to really help the lessons sink in.

Merchandise your success with this material. When you get a great idea, tell others about it. Tell them how you used Intergalactic Thinking or 180° Thinking to solve this or that challenge. When you become a champion for this type of thinking, it obligates you in a strong way to use the stuff. A little obligation may be all you need to stick with some of these new thinking methods when the deep memory of old patterns or attachment to old ideas tries to override even your most sincere efforts to be a fresh thinker.

Know that creative thinking is the only way to make anything better. And know that every big thinker in every area of endeavor had to break through the inertia of stagnant thinking to come up with a new idea.

I believe that true immortality comes about in two ways: through our children and through our new ideas. And in either case passion is the stuff that helps provide the spark.

Timeline of a great idea (continued)

Timeline of a lousy idea (continued)

"Grandpa, what did you used to
do for a living? Grandpa, those
    aren't tears, are they?"

Cheat Notes for Chapter 22:
Proceed with Passion

- Surround yourself with people who have passion for creative pursuits.

- Become a student of creativeness.

- Celebrate your own success.

- Study, study, study.

- Play in greener pastures.

- Practice, practice, practice.

- Use this stuff tomorrow.

- Use the cheat notes.

- Merchandise your success with this material.

Afterword

The Do-It-Yourself Lobotomy Early Years

In the spirit of 180° Thinking, I'd like to end this book at the beginning.

People often ask how long I've been practicing many of the habits and tools covered in this book. To be honest, I don't know.

I do know that I had some great early encouragement from my parents, particularly my mother. One story you'll like recalls the time my mom let my brother and me create our own wallpaper.

Like lots of boys growing up in the 1950s, we had cowboy wallpaper. I can vividly recall the classic images of various cowpokes in their leather chaps and broad-brimmed hats, alternating with images of cacti, horses, and the occasional three-rail fence.

I can also recall the graffiti brother Mike and I festooned on these innocent images. A wisecrack dialogue box here, an extra appendage there. (Did I mention we were, like, 12 and 13 years old?)

Well, my mom did what any mom would have done. Any mom who wanted to nurture the creativity in her children, that is. She said, "Boys, I'd like to do your walls over. But since we can't afford new wallpaper, particularly if you're going to continue defacing it, I'll paint the walls a neutral color and let you create your own wall covering." (Managers take note.)

So brother Mike and I went to town designing our own custom wallpaper. Well, we didn't design anything, really. In fact, this may have been where I learned the lesson to actually think through what you're going to create before you create it.

We had one drawing of our parish priest laid out in a coffin. (In actuality, he wasn't yet dead, which most definitely proved we had imaginations. It probably proved other things that only Freud could deduce.) We had a drawing of a teacher from school with his head in a guillotine. And these were the more positive images. (Only kidding.)

Is this a demonstration of creativity at an early age? Have I mentioned yet the correlation between creativity and dementia? Maybe that will be my next book.

I only wish we had taken pictures of that wall for documentation of my early training in this area of creative exploration.

BIG LESSON FROM LITTLE BROTHER

My brother Michael was born with a hole in his head. It was his mouth.

When brother Mike, 13 months my junior, was drawing at the kitchen table as a youngster, you never had to guess what he was drawing. You could always *hear* what he was putting down on paper.

If Michael was drawing a farm, the rest of the family could tell from two rooms away. "Oink! Oink!" we'd all hear, or "Moooo!" or "Cluck, cluck, cluck."

If we heard "Pow!!! Boom!!! Pow!!!" or "Bang, bang, bang, bang, bang," we knew Michael was drawing a war scene.

Then there were the times we'd hear "Oink, oink, POW!" Oh no, Michael's blowing up pigs.

What was the lesson I got from this innocent (?) little exercise my younger brother did daily with his crayons? You have to let it out. You can't keep it inside you.

> *When you're creating, you have to risk looking or sounding a little foolish, and you have to let it out.*

So often when leading brainstorming sessions or playing the "Guess my socks" game or some other in-room exercise at my training programs, I can see it in people's eyes that they're holding back. I can see the excitement of having a wild idea battling with the self-consciousness of exposing one's inner whims.

Every great thinker of every great idea has faced the moment when he or she had to make the decision to go public with their concept or to hold back. We should all be grateful that so many people have the guts to let those wonderful ideas out. Conversely, imagine how many great ideas have been lost on the tip of someone's mind, pen, paintbrush or keyboard.

Fortunately, I had my brother and his 80-decibel Crayolas to help me learn that important lesson early in life: If you don't let ideas out, no one will ever know what's on your mind.

180° WEDDING DAY

One early example of my use of these tools was on my wedding day. A mere 20 years old, and my bride, Audrey, even younger, we exhibited clear 180° Thinking in choosing the setting for our official wedding album photos.

I figured, "Hey, everybody shoots their wedding pictures at a park or in a garden, always someplace serene and beautiful. So why not do something at the far other end of the spectrum?" (I had not yet unveiled the term *180° Thinking*.) "Why not go to a dump?"

Well, thankfully, I didn't go with my first idea and we didn't go to a dump to take the photographs that were to document this most important day. We went to a salvage yard.

The National Wrecking Company in Pawtucket, Rhode Island, became the canvas upon which we asked our friend and soon-to-be-brother-in-law Jon McNally to capture the spirit of this special day. The various backdrops, besides the old furnace section of the salvage

yard shown here, included the bathtub, sink, and toilet departments, and that was just the bathroom section.

Did I mention my father-in-law did not get out of the car for a single photo?

Toward the end of the photo session we decided to take a "straight" shot for the last page of the wedding album, if taking a straight photo is at all possible in a salvage yard.

Did I mention it was a steamy August 29 around high noon? Can you imagine what a hot August 29 around high noon smells like in a salvage yard?

We all lined up in a clearing at the center of the parking lot for the formal wedding party photograph shown here.

$180° + 180° ≠ 360°$

To demonstrate that she was second to no one when it came to 180° Thinking, and to further set the tone for what has become a fun, creative marriage (31 years and counting), Audrey trumped me with the suggestion for the last, final photo for the wedding album.

The photograph on page 260, a 180° version of the straight shot, became the exclamation mark at the end of our photo album. I have chosen it as the punctuation for the end of this book.

The Beginning.

Appendix

EXHIBIT 1:
The 2-Minute Creative IQ Test™ for Individuals

Learn about your creative strengths and weaknesses. Your results will help you prioritize your reading. (Take the test below or go to www.Do-It-YourselfLobotomy.com/book.)

"Creative IQ test, oh really?" you ask (with a little suspicion).

By creative IQ I mean "Imagination Quotient," the basic habits and practices that individuals exercise that lead to fresh ideas.

This test, which I have developed over the years, has been taken by more than 100,000 people throughout the world. The gauges used are modeled after common thinking habits of some of the greatest creative minds throughout history.

This test is designed to gauge your creativeness as an individual. On page 246 is another test to gauge the creativeness of your organization. Take this test for as many contexts as you please: your job, hobbies, family life, whatever.

If you take this *and* the organization test, I recommend that you take the organization version first.

This is a quick, universal test with fairly generalized results driven by the answers you provide. There is certainly a margin for error, and there are exceptions to almost every rule, creativeness being as elusive as it is. But there is more method to the madness than most people realize. And the feedback can be extremely valuable, particularly if you're honest with yourself in how you answer the questions, have an open mind, and are looking to improve your abilities in this area. This test cannot measure the creativeness of any specific idea, nor does it measure artistic talent.

So, give it a shot. The results will help you to identify what you need to work on as you read this book.

Simply circle the answer that most applies. Then tally your score at the end to see how you rate, followed by helpful suggestions on how to make necessary improvements. Better understanding your strengths and weaknesses will give you heightened insight into which sections of the book to focus on for the most favorable result.

A. Are you quick to find fault with ideas—your own or those of others?

    1. Almost always
    2. Often
    3. Occasionally
    4. Rarely
    5. Never

B. How frequently do you get attached to how things are done?

    1. Almost always
    2. Often
    3. Occasionally
    4. Rarely
    5. Never

C. How often do you hold back from mentioning ideas for fear of looking silly or being "wrong"?

    1. Almost always
    2. Often
    3. Occasionally
    4. Rarely
    5. Never

D. Do you ever have the tendency to stop at your first good idea?

    1. Almost always
    2. Often
    3. Occasionally
    4. Rarely
    5. Never

E. How many ideas do you tend to generate — good or bad — when
    tackling a project?

    1. 1 or 2
    2. 3–5
    3. 6–12
    4. 13–25
    5. More than 25

To tally your score simply add up the five values in your circled
answers, then read on to see how you rate and find helpful suggestions.

_____ total score

Scoring

Scores

24–25 = A+	Very, very good. You wouldn't want to help me write my next book, would you?
21–23 = A	Very good. You are very highly realized creatively. Or you cheated on the test.
19–20 = B+	Much better than average, but there are some areas where you could improve.
16–18 = B	Better than average, and enough room for improvement to take seriously.
14–15 = C+	Better than average, but just barely. It's very good that you're reading this book.
11–13 = C	Average. But in creative pursuits, average is not enough. Read intensively.
9–10 = D+	Below average. This book will help with the answers and with the questions.
5–8 = D	Well below average. You really need this book. Take the advice very seriously.
0–4 = F	Either you were too tough on yourself or you really, really need this book.

Responses and Recommendations

Question A: Are you quick to find fault with ideas, yours or
others?

Criticism comes easier than craftsmanship.
~Zeuxis (c. 400 B.C.)

Ideaconstrictor.

The gruesome, poisonous, kid-eating thing that lurks deep beneath your bed.

Have you ever seen the Gary Larsen cartoon where poor little Todd can't step foot on his bedroom floor for fear of the boa constrictor living under his bed?

There were monsters who used to terrorize me in my bedroom, too. I used to talk to the cowboys on the wallpaper (vintage 1950) for comfort.

I look back today and laugh. But then it was very real for me. It had me frozen in fear virtually every night. Ahh, childhood.

Many of the fears that prevent people from coming up with brilliant ideas are quite the same as those that haunted me and little Todd. While unfounded, they limit us greatly, preventing us from venturing out from the comfort and security of our emotional/intellectual bed.

Fear is one of the biggest creative inhibitors. Actually there are many fears that prevent us from being more creative. But the specific fear I'm talking about here is the fear of coming up with a bad idea. Or, perhaps even more frustrating, the fear of articulating an idea that others might think is bad. Ouch. (Did that hit close to home?)

Forget the subject of "what's bad," which is fodder of another chapter. Here the issue is letting our fear of bad ideas prevent us from even considering anything too out of the ordinary, a sure formula for the same old tired thinking.

Forget that you've heard that there is no such thing as a bad idea. There are plenty of things in the world that are undisputed proof of the existence of bad ideas. You never bought that "no such thing as a bad idea" crap anyway, did you?

Yes, there are bad ideas. Yes. Yes. Absolutely. Yes. But that doesn't mean we need to be afraid of them. Because, no, a bad idea is not harmful. Not harmful at all. (Beware: this scary story is continued on the following spread.)

During the fragile early stages of the creative process is not the time to test an idea's validity. Almost all new ideas have flaws. When you're too quick to judge, you often overlook what's worthwhile and drag down the entire creative process. Even if an idea isn't perfect, it's more constructive to look at what's good about it and keep making it better rather than to take the easy way out and drag it down.

If your answer is *almost always* or *often,* judgment is a problem area for you. You're much too judgmental when it comes to new ideas. Try to be more conscious of premature judgment and hold off as long as you can. If you don't improve here you seriously risk any consistent creative success. When you judge others' ideas, you risk alienating them and losing them as creative collaborators.

If your answer to question A is *occasionally* or *rarely,* you are sometimes judgmental when it comes to new ideas. Try to be more conscious of premature judgment and hold off evaluation as long as you can. You might be surprised at how many ideas look better in the light of a new day. You have nothing to lose and a great deal to gain.

If your answer to question A is *never,* this is an area of strength for you. It appears that you are not prone to quick negative judgments of new ideas as are most people.

Question B: How frequently do you get attached to how things are done?

> *Change your thoughts and you change your world.*
> ~Norman Vincent Peale

When people are attached to how things are done, it means that they are not looking for better ways to do things. Resistance to change holds back progress and puts you in a compromising competitive position. Change is inevitable in every area of endeavor. Your field has likely undergone much change in the past, which needs to be recognized.

One sure way to avoid resisting change is to actually effect it! That's certainly what high achievers do.

If your answer is *almost always* or *often,* this is a problem area for you, as you're quite resistant to change and are much too attached to how things are done. You are missing major opportunities to improve things by being too attached to how things are done. You likely avoid the kinds of risk that change entails. But being as stuck as you are creates an even greater risk: being left behind by a world that *is* changing. You need to improve in this area for your very survival.

(scary story continued from previous spread) "Excuse me?" you ask, with just a hint of skepticism.

Ideas are benign. As unthreatening as the little, yellow, kitten that used to sleep under the sofa of the little old lady who lived next door.

Even the worst, stupidest, most potentially disastrous ideas are absolutely, totally, harmless. And the key word here is potentially. You see, ideas are harmless because they are not real. Yet, that is. They are only potentially real. As ideas, they are products of our imagination. Like Todd's snakes. Like those monsters that had me talking to the wallpaper. Unlike Todd's snakes and my monsters, ideas can become real. All someone has to do is execute the idea, and it's real, But until it's executed it's only a harmless, silly little idea.

But we're afraid of ideas that are different. Ideas that are new, mysterious, unproven. And we're afraid of the reaction we might get from others who are afraid of them. "Are you crazy?" "That type of thing will never work." "That's dumb."

And we and the other detractors fail to realize that it's only an idea. We haven't risked anything yet by thinking about it. We haven't stuck our necks out. We haven't bet the ranch. We just formulated a concept that may or may not materialize. No harm. No need to worry. It's only an idea. A meek, little, fuzzy, brand-spankin' newborn kitten of an idea.

We need to learn this lesson. And those around us need to learn this same lesson. You know, our supposed support system.

Lesson: Listen to FDR: The only thing we have to fear is fear itself.

If your answer is *occasionally* or *rarely*, you are sometimes resistant to change and can be attached to how things are done. Perhaps you are a victim of your own success. When something works, people resist changing, but in so doing they are likely only holding back improvement.

If your answer is *never*, this is an area of strength for you. It appears you are not nearly as resistant to change as most people. But there is one caution for people who score high in this area. When you answer that you are not attached to how things are done, are you talking about your habits now or in your glory days? Many people who achieve creative breakthroughs early in their careers or lives think of themselves as creative, then go on to continually emulate their early success. Alfred Hitchcock said that style is self-plagiarism. Beware of this trap. Are you a victim of your own success?

When something works successfully people resist changing, but in so doing they are only holding back from further creative accomplishment.

Question C: How often do you hold back from mentioning ideas for fear of looking silly or being wrong?

> *Those who do not stop asking silly questions become scientists.*
> ~Leon Lederman, nuclear physicist

Sticking your neck out with a new idea means taking a risk, but without some risk there are few advancements. We've been trained since our early years to "make sense" and to "not look foolish." Logic, rational thinking and linear thought have been drilled into us. Even the standard IQ test mostly measures convergent thinking. But the greatest thinkers of all time were often divergent thinkers. New ideas often don't make sense and might sound silly or wrong. Often, crazy ideas are a lot closer to brilliant than the same tired old "this is the way it is" ideas.

If your answer is *almost always* or *often*, this is a problem area for you, as it appears you're very apprehensive about mentioning new ideas to others. This is not uncommon, but it hurts your creative achievement. New ideas often don't make sense in the current order of things. Your self-consciousness keeps you in the realm of "what is" and prevents you from exploring "what might be better."

If your answer is *occasionally* or *rarely*, it appears you are sometimes apprehensive about mentioning new ideas to others. Keep in mind that new ideas frequently don't make much sense in the current order of things. Your self-consciousness might keep you in the realm of "what is" and prevent you from exploring "what might be better," thus hampering your creative achievement.

If your answer is *never*, congratulations. Based on your answer in this area, it appears you are entirely uninhibited when it comes to mentioning new ideas to others. This will serve you well in areas of creative pursuit. You are likely a very open, creative individual who knows that not all new ideas sound brilliant, and you are willing to take the chance of appearing silly or wrong. Either that, or you work in a very supportive, open-minded environment.

Question D: Do you ever have the tendency to stop at your first good idea?

> *Good is the enemy of great.*
> ~Voltaire

It's quite natural for people to stop at their first good idea. But when you do this early on in the creative process you are limiting the possibility of an even better idea materializing. One way to discourage stopping at your first good idea is to work quickly during the early ideation phase and simply keep judgment out of the process. If you don't judge, you don't know what's good or bad, so you don't become attached to the "good," stop ideating, and prevent yourself from finding something even better.

If your answer is *almost always* or *often*, this is a problem area for you since you tend to stop at your first good idea much too often. You need to change your habits in this area; otherwise, you're likely just putting all of your effort into executing mediocre ideas.

If your answer is *occasionally* or *rarely*, you tend to stop at your first good idea a bit more often than you should. Remember, when you do this early on in the creative process you are preventing the possibility of an even better idea being born.

If your answer is *never*, it appears you are not prone to stopping at your first good idea, as are most people. Keep it up!

Question E: How many ideas do you tend to generate—good or bad—when tackling a project?

> *I have lots of ideas.*
> ~Linus Pauling, two-time Nobel laureate
> (when asked to explain why he had such great ideas)

Yes, when you brainstorm you're usually looking for *the* idea. But a big part of creativity is simply a numbers game. Generate more ideas and you'll simply have more ideas from which to choose the best. You'll have more good ideas and, sure, more bad ideas. But bad ideas can often be fertilizer for the creative process. The best creative thinkers produce more fertilizer than most people. (Maybe that's how they got to be great thinkers.)

If your answer is *1 or 2* or *3–5*, this is a problem area for you since you are not generating anywhere near enough quantity of ideas to better ensure a high-quality outcome. Remember that bad ideas can be fertilizer. Using quantity to get to quality is one of the easiest ways to overachieve creatively. Most great thinkers were prolific ideators. Plus, it diffuses that destructive judgment element.

If your answer is *6–12* or *13–25*, you are generating as many or more ideas than the average person, but could push it even further to better ensure a higher-quality result. Keep in mind that in areas of creative pursuit, quantity usually leads to quality.

If your answer is *more than 25*, you are ready, willing, and able to generate many fresh ideas. You probably generate a lot of fertilizer, too.

If you haven't already checked it out, you may want to explore the Creative IQ test for organizations below.

EXHIBIT 2:
The 2-Minute Creative IQ Test for Organizations

This is a quick, universal test that I have developed to help managers gauge the creativeness of their organizations: entire companies, departments, work groups, or teams. You can take the test here or go to www.Do-It-YourselfLobotomy.com/book. The test offers fairly generalized results, driven by the answers you provide. The gauges used are modeled after common thinking habits of some of the greatest creative minds throughout history. There is certainly a margin for error, and exceptions to almost every rule, creativeness being as elusive as it is. But the feedback can be extremely valuable, particularly if you're honest with yourself in answering the questions, have an open mind, and are looking to improve your abilities in this area. This test cannot measure the creativeness of any specific idea, nor does it measure artistic talent.

As with the test for individuals, simply circle the most applicable answer. Then tally your score at the end. You'll see how your group rates, followed by helpful suggestions for improvement. As with the test for individuals, better understanding of the creative strength and weaknesses, in this case relating to your organization, will give you heightened insight into which sections of the book you should focus on for the most favorable result. No matter how your group scores, you'll find additional valuable insights into managing people for optimal creative output in Chapter 18, "Mind Farming."

A. Are the people in your organization quick to find fault with new ideas?

1. Always
2. Very often
3. Frequently
4. Sometimes
5. Never

B. How many of the people in your group are attached to how things are done?

1. All
2. Most
3. Many
4. Some
5. None

C. How often do your managers bring out fresh thinking in their people?

1. Never
2. Sometimes
3. Frequently
4. Very often
5. Always

D. How often do the people in your organization stop at their first good idea?

1. Always
2. Very often
3. Frequently
4. Sometimes
5. Never

E. How many ideas—good and bad (even those you discount immediately)—are generated by people in your group during a typical brainstorming session?

1. 10 or less
2. 11–25
3. 26–50

> 4. 51–99
> 5. 100 and more

To tally your score, simply add up the five values in your circled answers, then read on to see how you rate and find helpful suggestions.

_____total score

Scoring

Please note that this quick survey is an inexact process. Depending on the validity of your answers, this can give you strong indicators about what is working and what isn't working in your organization.

Scores

24–25 = A+ Very, very good. You work for an amazingly creative organization. Either that or you find it impossible to be objective about your group's flaws.

21–23 = A Very good. Your group is very highly realized creatively. Can I come work for you?

19–20 = B+ Much better than average, but there are some areas in which your group could improve.

16–18 = B Better than average, and enough room for improvement to take seriously.

14–15 = C+ Better than average, but just barely. It's very good that you're reading this book.

11–13 = C Average. But in creative pursuits, average is not enough. Read intensively.

9–10 = D+ Below average. You might suggest others in your company read this book.

5–8 = D Well below average. I'd insist that everyone in your group read this book.

0–4 = F Either you were too tough on your group, you really, really need this book, or you ought to look for work in a company that has a clue, creatively.

Responses and Recommendations

Question A: Are the people in your organization quick to find fault with new ideas?

There's a time to find fault with ideas. The fragile early stages of the creative process is not the proper time. Almost all ideas have some flaws. When people are too quick to judge, they often overlook what's worthwhile about an idea and drag down the entire creative process. Even if an idea isn't perfect, it's much more constructive to look at what's good about it and keep making it better rather than to take the easy way out and drag it down.

If your answer to question A was *always* or *very often,* your people are much too judgmental when it comes to new ideas. Even if you answered *frequently* or *sometimes,* judgment is an area of some concern for your group. To help your people be more conscious of their potentially destructive judgment, you might consider using sportslike penalty flags in meetings or just politely call one another on such behavior. If your company doesn't improve in this area you risk demotivating your best thinkers or even losing them.

If you answered *never,* it appears your people are not prone to quick negative judgments of new ideas as are most people in industry. Congratulations!

Question B: How many of the people in your group are attached to how things are done?

When people are attached to how things are done, they miss major opportunities for improvement. This holds back progress and puts your company in a compromising competitive position. Change is inevitable in any organization and industry. Your company has likely undergone much change in the past, which needs to be recognized. One sure way to avoid resisting change is to actually effect it! That's certainly what leading companies do.

If your answer to question B was *all* or *most,* your people are quite resistant to change and are too attached to how things are done. Your people likely avoid the kinds of risk that change entails. But being as stuck as they are creates an even greater risk, being left behind by others who do change, because any advancement requires change. You need to improve in this area for your company's very survival.

If your answer to question B was *many* or *some,* your people are occasionally resistant to change and are likely attached to how things are done. Or perhaps your people are victims of their own success. When something works, people resist changing it, but in so doing they are likely only holding back improvement.

If your answer was *none,* it appears that your people are not as resistant to change as most people in industry. Count your blessings.

Question C: How often do your managers bring out fresh thinking in their people?

Managers need to know that their people are usually only as creative as their managers allow or encourage them to be. To put a lid on the staff's creative output in any way is starving the organization of a much needed energy supply.

If your answer to question C was *never* or *sometimes,* your managers could do a much better job of bringing out creativity in others. Based on your answer in this area, your managers might be more than weak in this area—they could even be an *impediment.* It appears that your managers might actually provide discouragement, a big no-no. Putting a lid on the staff's creative output starves the organization of your best thinking. You have some serious work to do in this area. Some easy first steps are (1) being more open to new thinking and (2) actually asking for it.

If your answer was *frequently* or *very often,* your managers could still do a better job of bringing out creativity in others. To reiterate, some easy steps to higher performance in this area are (1) being more open to new thinking and (2) actually asking for it.

If your answer was *always,* congratulations. It appears your managers are excellent at bringing out creative thinking in others.

Question D: How often do the people in your organization stop at their first good idea?

It's quite natural for people to stop at their first good idea. But when they do this early on in the creative process they are limiting the possibility of an even better idea materializing. One way to discourage stopping at the first good idea is to simply keep judgment out of the process during the early ideation phase. If you don't judge, you don't know what's good or bad, so you don't get attached to the "good," stop ideating, and prevent yourself from finding something even better.

If your answer to question D was *always* or *very often,* this is a problem area, because too many of your people stop at their first good idea too often. Your group needs to change its habits in this area; otherwise, you risk putting too much of your effort into executing mediocre ideas.

If your answer was *frequently* or *sometimes,* too many people in your group tend to stop at their first good idea a bit more often than they should.

If your answer was *never,* it appears that your people are not prone to stopping at their first good idea, as are most people. That's great!

Question E: How many ideas—good and bad (even those you discount immediately)—are generated by people in your group during a typical brainstorming session?

Yes, when you brainstorm you're usually looking for *the* idea. But a big part of creativity is simply a numbers game. Generate more ideas, and you'll simply have more ideas from which to choose the best. You'll have more good ideas and, sure, more bad ideas. But bad ideas can often be fertilizer for the creative process. The best creative thinkers produce more fertilizer than most people. (Maybe that's how they got to be great thinkers.)

If your answer to question E was *10 or less* or *11–25*, your people do not generate anywhere near enough quantity of ideas to ensure a high-quality outcome. Using quantity to get to quality is one of the easiest ways to get people to overachieve creatively. Plus, it minimizes that destructive judgment element. The same is true if your answer was *26–50* or *50–99*.

If your answer was *more than 100*, it appears your people are ready, willing, and able to generate many fresh ideas. They probably generate a lot of fertilizer, too. Your people are obviously high achievers.

EXHIBIT 3:
Creative ForceField Analysis

What's your Creative ForceField™? This is a quick self-assessment to help you better understand the forces that enable your creativeness and the forces that limit you in this area.

Your level of creative realization is a direct product of the conditions inside and outside of you that either contribute to your creative achievement or inhibit it. What are the forces helping you to be creative? What are the forces limiting you? These forces strongly influence your individual achievement on the job and elsewhere in life. If you understand them more clearly, you're in a better position to improve your creative ability.

Your Creative ForceField
When you complete the Creative ForceField on page 255 (or online at www.Do-It-YourselfLobotomy.com/book) you make a document that you can use personally to survey your own creative landscape as you begin the development of your creative skill set, which this book aims to help you do. You should address this exercise as it relates to you, not to others in your personal or work life, unless of course you are doing this for your organization, in which case you'll interpret the directions a bit differently. Please be candid and forthcoming, but also realistic

Neutral Creativity ForceField

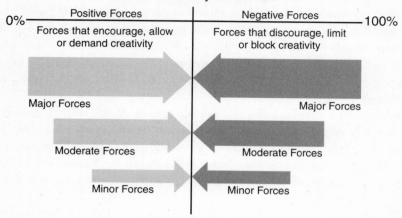

There are forces propelling you toward 100%
creative realization and forces repelling you from this
ultimate state of creativeness.

High-Functioning Creative State

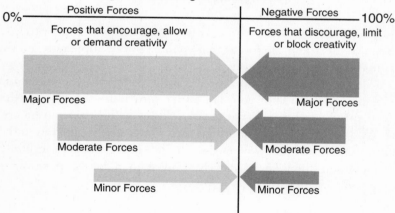

When you have more and larger forces on the
positive side of your Creative ForceField you are
more highly realized creatively.

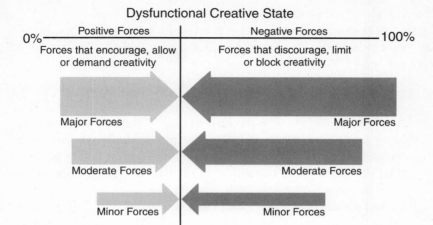

When you have more and larger forces on the
negative side of your Creative ForceField you are less
highly realized creatively.

about certain forces that are simply a part of your reality. I recommend
that you do this exercise before you get too far along in this book, and
also at the end to gauge your immediate progress. Periodically after
you have put to work some of the concepts and tools covered in this
book, come back and gauge your Creative ForceField again.

A Short Lesson on the Creative ForceField

Basically, we all have forces in our lives—at home, on the job, and
elsewhere—that help us achieve creativeness as well as forces working
against our creativity. The larger the number of positive forces you
have and the greater the strength of those forces in relation to the negative forces, the more highly realized you can become creatively. Conversely, the larger the number negative forces you have and the greater
the strength of those forces in relation to your positive forces, the more
stifled you are creatively.

The same goes for your company, department, or work group, your
family unit, your Thursday night jam session, and so on.

The objectives are quite simple. First, identify the forces working for
and against your creativeness. Once those forces have been identified,
use the insights and recommendations in this book to increase the positive forces or add additional positive forces. And, perhaps more important, use this book to help you work at diminishing the negative forces on
the other side of the energy field.

The result? More healthy conditions for creativity to flourish.

Plot Your Creative ForceField

On the worksheet chart your creative forces, positive and negative. And don't hold back. This instrument is most valuable if filled out fully and frankly.

> *Positive forces.* List the forces that promote, encourage, allow, or even demand creativity for you. They are inner-driven (e.g., natural curiosity) and outer-driven (e.g., "My boss expects it").
>
> *Negative forces.* List what discourages, limits, blocks, or prevents creativity for you. Again, these are things within you (e.g., "my fear of failure") and things less in your control (e.g., "risk aversion in others").
>
> *Magnitude counts.* Note, not all forces are equal. To help weight them I've provided three levels on each side: major, moderate, and minor.

Also note, we all have different Creative ForceFields in different areas: our jobs, our hobbies, our home life, and so on. Choose which Creative ForceField you want to focus on; that should be the one you measure in this exercise. But feel free to copy the worksheet and fill out multiple forms for different areas.

With or Without a Net?

You can fill this out totally unaided from your own introspection, or you can look at some frequently mentioned forces provided on our cheat sheet on page 256. If you do choose to use it, we recommend you do as much as possible unaided first, then apply your own specifics when using our cheat sheet to keep the assessment as true as possible.

Once you've completed your Creative ForceField, save it to document where you are at this point in time. This is your present reality and your road map for creative growth. What's within your control, and what's not? It's *all* in your control:

- Accentuate the positive.
- Add to the positive forces.
- On the negative side, eliminate, diminish, avoid, accept.

Creative ForceField Worksheet

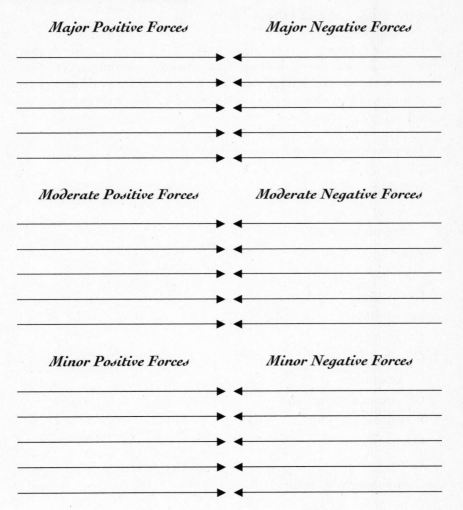

Major Positive Forces   **Major Negative Forces**

Moderate Positive Forces   **Moderate Negative Forces**

Minor Positive Forces   **Minor Negative Forces**

I suggest you copy this worksheet and fill out at least one copy before and after you read the book.

©Before & After, 1995.

Exhibit 4:
Creative ForceField Cheat Sheet

Warning: It's important to use this list only as a prompt for forces that really exist in your life. This is not a place to add something to your list because it sounds good. Also note that these items are listed in no particular order and without regard to magnitude. Most of these forces are stated in very general terms.

Frequently Mentioned Positive Forces

Encouragement from teacher(s)

Permission from parents

A strong nurturing mentor

World experiences

Reading

Traveling

Challenges

Recognition

Empowerment

Ownership

Collaboration

Corporate environment

People I work with

Competition

Exercise

Communing with nature

Exposure to the arts

Freedom to fail

Working under pressure

Open-minded people (specify)

Frequently Mentioned Negative Forces

Closed-minded people (specify)

Need to be right

Not enough money

Too much time

Not enough time

Poor direction

Vague objectives

Little tolerance for mistakes or failure

When people don't care

Corporate environment

Low budget

Other's arbitrary constraints

Politics

Meetings

Interruptions

Fear

EXHIBIT 5:
Solution to the Nine-Dot Test on Page 107

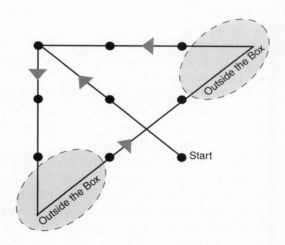

EXHIBIT 6:
Suggested Reading List

This is obviously only a partial list. More and more books have been
written on this topic in recent years. In addition to books specifically
about creativity, I also suggest reading biographies of high-achieving
people in your field and, particularly, in other fields of endeavor.

A Whack on the Side of the Head and *A Kick in the Seat of the Pants* by
   Roger Von Oech. This guy has done a better job of packaging
   "creative understanding" for general consumption than anyone in
   this country in our time.
A Creative Companion and *Inspiration Sandwich* by Sark. A couple of
   delightful little books with more gems of thoughts than words
   (figure *that* out).
The Creative Spirit by Daniel Goleman, Paul Kaufman, and Michael
   Ray. This is the companion piece to a PBS series on creativity.
   Quick, light reading. And like all of these, chock-full of wisdom
   on the subject.
A Technique for Producing Ideas by James Webb Young. A one-hour
   read, this little book provides a useful, easy, effective technique
   for producing ideas.
Most any book by Edward duBono, although *Lateral Thinking* is the
   only one I've been able to make real sense of so far. Then again,
   I can often be pretty thick.
The Secret Language of the Mind by David Cohen. This is a wonderfully designed book about many aspects of the mind: memory,
   dreams, vision, and more. The explanations are as much visual
   as verbal.
The Act of Creation, 750 mind-numbing pages, by Arthur Koestler.
   Long, yes, but long on lessons, too.
The Art of Creativity by Wilfred Petterson. A wonderful book that
   offers a chapter per spread on different aspects of creativity, by
   a guy who really makes this crazy stuff seem simple.
The Magic of Thinking Big by David Schwartz. The most Dale
   Carnegie-esque of the lot. But full of useful tidbits.
How the Mind Works by Steven Pinker. This MIT professor tackles
   an enormous topic and makes it fairly understandable to the
   average reader.

More Specific to Writing

    Wild Mind and *Writing Down the Bones* by Natalie Goldberg. Is she talking about creativity or is she talking about life? And how different are they anyway?

More Specific to Advertising

    Hey Whipple, Squeeze This by Luke Sullivan. A wonderful book packed with insight and practical advice on how to create great advertising by a copywriter who has been there. Plus, it's funny as hell.

More Specific to Design

    Problem: Solution by Richard Wilde and *Visual Literacy* by Richard and Judith Wilde. An absolute must for graphic-oriented communications from the chairman of the advertising and design departments of the acclaimed School for Visual Arts in New York City and his equally adept wife.

Additional Study

For periodic updates to this reading list, go to www.Do-It-YourselfLobotomy.com/reading.html.

For experiential professional development workshops in various areas of creative thinking, go to www.creative-camp.com/events.html.

For corporate professional development programs and brainstorm facilitating, go to www.before-after.com.

See 180° wedding day story on page 236.

Acknowledgments

First I'd like to thank Pat Briden, my business manager and herder of the many cats that can be me. Pat's role in the development and writing of this book was absolutely invaluable. She provided the first wave of editorial comment at almost every stage, performed research, chased down the permissions, created the index, and did most of the many technical illustrations.

I'd also like to thank all the people and companies whose stories and creative output helped me articulate and illustrate so many of the points that needed to be made in this book.

Let me also thank my agent Michael Cohn, Andrew Jaffe at Adweek Books, and executive editor Airié Dekidjiev at John Wiley & Sons for seeing the value of this book long before it took final form. Plus all the other people at John Wiley & Sons and North Market Street Graphics who contributed to bringing this book to life, especially Chris Furry.

Dan Madole gets my sincere thanks for his design of this book's dust jacket, as do my friends at Magical Monkey for their early cover design work. Thanks also to Mary Sward for providing editorial guidance in my very early writings that provided the foundation for some of this book.

Thanks, too, to all the companies and professional organizations who have hired Before & After, Inc.™ over the years and all the individuals who participated in the many workshops and brainstorming sessions I've conducted, plus all the individuals who have attended my creative camps. All of these people and organizations have helped me better understand creativity as they have allowed me to help them explore this wonderful stuff and put it to work for them.

Additionally, I'd like to thank the people who have had the greatest impact on my creative and professional trajectory: my parents, Tom and Pearl Monahan, and other family members, the Beatles, Jimi Hendrix and all the creative influences from my youth, Ernie Schenck, my rock bandmate and advertising colleague for many years, my early employers who first gave me a shot at applying my professional creative energy, plus my partners and the many employees at Leonard/Monahan and all of our clients who provided great encouragement and inspiration with their shared belief in the power of great ideas. Of this last group I'd like to single out Bruce Leonard, my most valued mentor, who taught me more about business than anyone else, and whose vision, creativeness, and belief in my ideas and capabilities inspired me and has given me the courage to make many of the most significant professional leaps I've made in my career.

Finally, a special thank you to my wonderful wife, Audrey, and tremendous daughter, Hillary, for sharing with me the most important creative exploration of all, life.

Index